A Father's Double Life

(New Edited Edition)

Michael Cavicante

authorHOUSE®

AuthorHouse™
1663 Liberty Drive
Bloomington, IN 47403
www.authorhouse.com
Phone: 1-800-839-8640

© 2011 Michael Cavicante. All rights reserved.

No part of this book may be reproduced, stored in a retrieval system, or transmitted by any means without the written permission of the author.

First published by AuthorHouse 6/15/2011

ISBN: 978-1-4634-0647-9 (e)
ISBN: 978-1-4634-0646-2 (dj)
ISBN: 978-1-4634-0648-6 (sc)

Library of Congress Control Number: 2011908728

Printed in the United States of America

Any people depicted in stock imagery provided by Thinkstock are models, and such images are being used for illustrative purposes only. Certain stock imagery © Thinkstock.

Because of the dynamic nature of the Internet, any web addresses or links contained in this book may have changed since publication and may no longer be valid. The views expressed in this work are solely those of the author and do not necessarily reflect the views of the publisher, and the publisher hereby disclaims any responsibility for them.

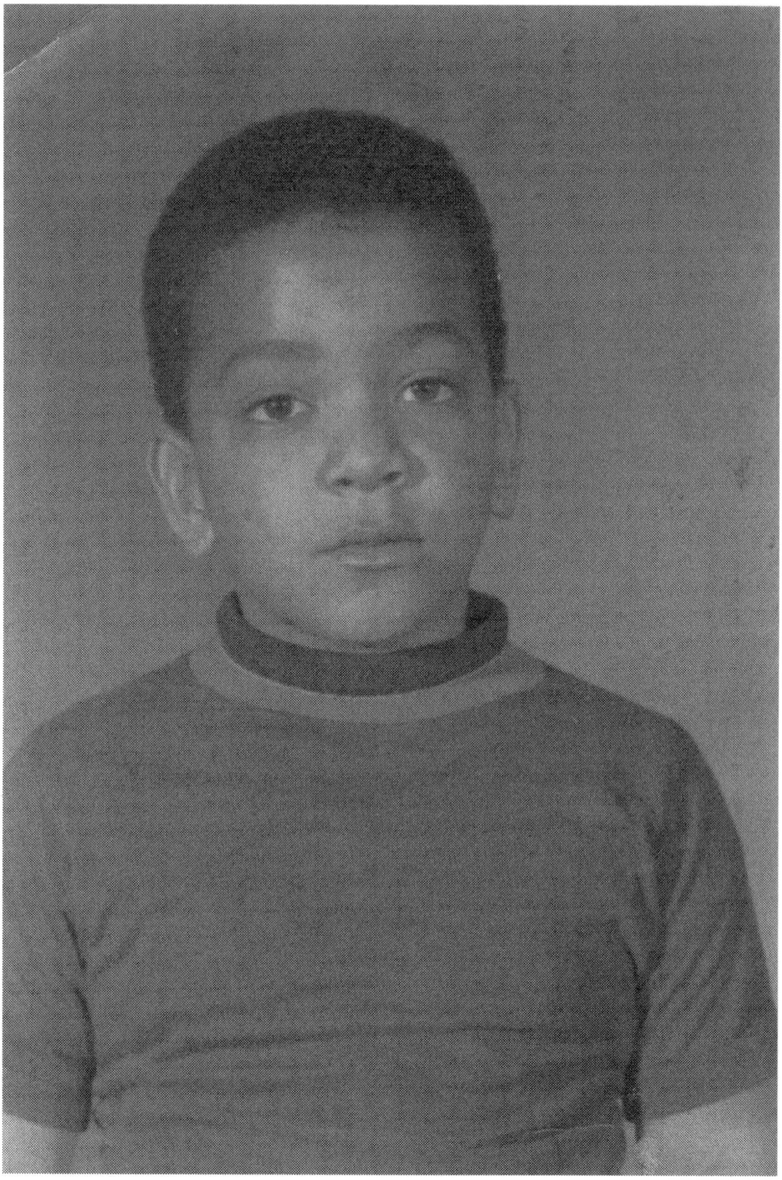

DEDICATION

I DEDICATE THIS BOOK TO MY mother, who throughout her life has been the best mother that any child could ever have. It is because of her, that I was able to survive the first twenty years of my life, as she was the only thing that I had to look forward to when everything else seemed to be going wrong; she was always the light at the end of the tunnel. I admire her in so many ways, mainly because she has struggled all her life, but yet still, wakes up everyday with a smile on her face and says "Everything is going to be alright."

She was against me writing this book, but she told me that if it was going to be good therapy for me, then to go ahead and write it. She was worried about the legacy of the Cavicante name and what this book would do to that legacy. I told her that as long as she carried the Cavicante name, there is no way on earth that the legacy of the Cavicante name could ever be ruined.

My mother is a great woman and loved by many. We say that judgment lies with our creator, God, and therefore Jesus Christ our savior, but I know that I can safely say for a certainty, that if any one person deserves a place in Heaven, it is my mother, **Juanita Maria Cavicante**.

It is with these words, that I totally, completely and solely, dedicate this book in your memory. You have truly been a blessing to me as a mother as I am sure that you have equally been an inspiration to every life you have ever touched along the way, and **I LOVE YOU DEARLY!!!**

PREFACE

This is the story of how I, as a boy, overcame obstacle after obstacle to become a man. You will experience everything that I did throughout my childhood years as no stones will be left unturned. I will go into every detail about the childhood years of my life.

I have often been told that my life is an open book. Well, it has literally become one. You will find that I experienced many things before my twentieth birthday and I was forced to grow up quickly while making my childhood years as if they never existed.

I wanted to write this book because a lot of people that I meet assume that I have always had a good life, that I came from a good upbringing and have never struggled, that my parents must have been great and that I had no worries as a child. They look at me and say, *"He's never had it bad,"* but little do they know the trials and tribulations I went through as a child and what I endured to become the person I am today.

I wanted to write this book because I hear of so many young people in their late teens to early mid-twenties that complain about their childhood and use it as an excuse as to why they are dealing and/or doing drugs, in and out of jail, stealing, killing and destroying their lives as well as the people around them. I say to you that there is no excuse and if you want a better life for yourself then you can make it happen, but only you can make it happen and no one else.

This story is told in chronological order from my birth. I hope you enjoy it.

Contents

Chapter 1	Beaned Out	1
Chapter 2	Life Goes On	11
Chapter 3	Having Faith	23
Chapter 4	Nine lives going fast	31
Chapter 5	Embarrassing Moments	39
Chapter 6	A Father's Betrayal	49
Chapter 7	Downward Spiral	57
Chapter 8	The Dallas Effect	63
Chapter 9	Freshman Year	73
Chapter 10	Lesson Not Learned	79
Chapter 11	A Mother's Devastation	85
Chapter 12	Back to Court	93
Chapter 13	The Runaway	97
Chapter 14	Verdict is in	105
Chapter 15	Blue Balls	111
Chapter 16	Lights Out	121
Chapter 17	Pac Man Fever	127
Chapter 18	Determined to Work	133
Chapter 19	Not Again	141
Chapter 20	Loophole	149

Chapter 21	Car Notes	157
Chapter 22	Imaginary Sex	165
Chapter 23	Senior Year Finale'	173
Chapter 24	Summer School	179
Chapter 25	Career Decision	183
Chapter 26	Bon Voyage	195
Chapter 27	Flashbacks	203
Chapter 28	A Different Kind of Smoker	209
A Mother's Love		215

Chapter 1
Beaned Out

THE UNITED STATES IS IN the middle of the Vietnam War as American Troops escalate to 250,000; Texas Western upset the Kentucky Wildcats to be the first NCAA Basketball Team to win the National Championship by starting an all African-American starting line-up; Fidel Castro declares Martial Law; Dr. Martin Luther King Junior is leading the Civil Rights Movement; Actor Ronald Reagan is elected Governor of California; Walt Disney Dies; Mass Murderer Richard Speck is arrested; the Beatles perform their last concert at Candlestick Park in San Francisco and Lyndon B. Johnson is President; the year—1966.

It would only be fitting, that amidst the chaos, controversy, prejudice and wars, I, Michael Cavicante, would be born to Raymond and Juanita, at Los Angeles County General Hospital, February 28th the same year. I was the second of three kids they would have together, as my older brother was born just eleven months earlier, April 8th, 1965.

Three years removed from my mother's womb, she decided that she didn't want her kids raised in such a big city, so the five of us boarded a train and arrived in the great state of Tennessee. She was pregnant with a third child.

We moved next door to the wicked witch, into a roach infested, four-room duplex on East Trigg Avenue in South Memphis in 1969. You will find out who the wicked witch is shortly.

Memphis was a relatively small city, but becoming famous due to it being the home of Elvis Presley at the time, but also infamous, because it

Michael Cavicante

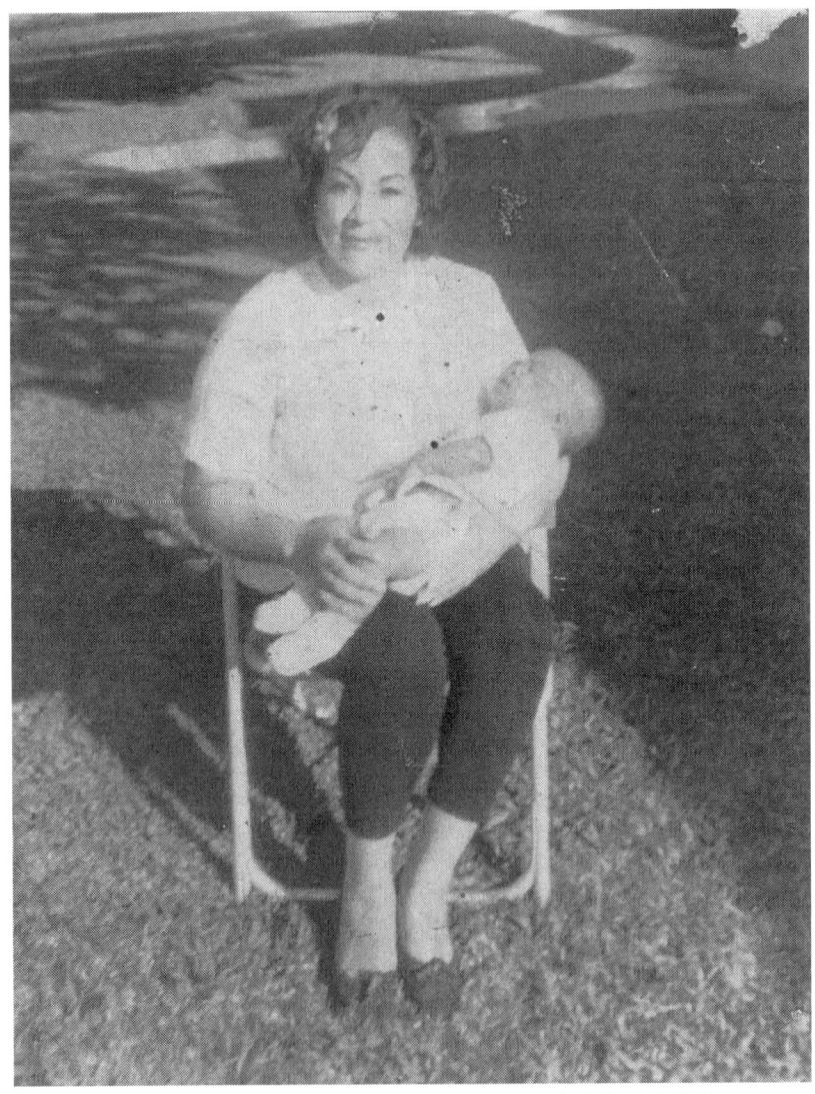

MY MOTHER WHILE STILL IN LOS ANGELES AS SHE
IS HOLDING MY OLDER BROTHER ROBIN, BUT ALSO
PREGNANT WITH ME IN THIS LATE 1965 PICTURE

was the city in which civil rights leader, Reverend Martin Luther King was assassinated just a year prior, in 1968.

The house itself had a living room, bedroom, kitchen and a bathroom. The home might have been six hundred square feet at best. The walls were some hideous shade of green and the ceilings were cracking all over, looking as if they would fall at any time. The floor was covered with cheap linoleum that was peeling up from the floor, just enough that one would trip over it, if not watching where they were going.

The front yard was big enough to change your mind if you needed to and the front porch was made of rotting wooden slats and also looked as if termites were eating away at it before my very eyes. The backyard was nothing more than dirt with little to no grass and a stoop off of the back door that had three steps.

The outside of the home wasn't brick, stucco, wood or siding. It was like roofing material and therefore resembled asbestos shingles. I occasionally tore a piece off the side of the house and slung it like a boomerang once or twice.

The style of house was called a shotgun house, which by definition meant that you could stand at the front door with a shotgun, aim at the back door straight ahead only sixty feet away, shoot and the pellets would go straight through and out the rear of the house, without touching anything else. That was where we lived for the next several years.

I saw rats or mice scurrying across the floor every so often, and again. Roaches were the norm. So normal in fact, that I woke up some mornings with one sitting on my pillow and staring me right in the eye as if to say,

"Good Morning."

The roaches were so bad that I had awful dreams they were crawling all over me and woke up only to find out that the dreadful dream was my reality as I brushed them off of my arms and legs, totally freaking out at times while yelling and screaming. At that point, my mother would run into the room and hold me while I fell to sleep in her arms as she sang The Carpenters' song, *"Close to You".*

The song was beautiful, and the lyrics along with her melodic voice always soothed me. These were the little things that my mother did to ease any hurt, pain, or otherwise, in order to comfort me in the time of need.

Born in 1935, my mother was of Irish/Black descent. She was fair skinned and therefore, people didn't know what to make of her, but she was accepted by most as being white. Though full-figured, she was very pretty and had hazel eyes that changed colors. She also had a particularly outgoing personality and was liked by everyone that she met.

Michael Cavicante

THIS IS MY FATHER WHILE STILL LIVING IN LOS
ANGELES IN THIS 1960'S PHOTOGRAPH

A Father's Double Life

Shortly after arriving in Memphis, my father went on to finish trucking school and was hired by some small firm as a truck driver, while my mother worked at Hyde Park laundry.

My father, born in San Francisco in 1927, was of Italian descent. He had jet black, wavy hair, which was also curly at the ends. He was five foot seven inches tall, slender and had the customary, heavy, Italian eyebrows and mustache; he was also accepted as Caucasian. I must say that my father was a very handsome man and knew it.

He had very few bad habits and was extremely meticulous and an anal-retentive. He kept his nails trimmed and stayed in the mirror primping. He couldn't pass a mirror without looking into it. When at home and not asleep, he planted himself on the couch, no matter where we were living. Everything had its place on the coffee table in front of him as his cigarettes and lighter was neatly arranged, along with his ashtray.

He also loved drinking milk from the container while standing at the refrigerator, which was probably the only bad habit he had, next to smoking cigarettes that is. All in all, he was a hard worker while seemingly wanting better for us to a degree and, therefore, tried to be a devoted father.

While my father was busy primping in the mirror, I was introduced to my Aunt Mattie who just so happened to be in Memphis on a visit from her home in Kansas City, Missouri. She was actually my great aunt and the sister of my grandfather John, who she was visiting.

Aunt Mattie was a very pretty, light-skinned, of average size, black lady. When about to leave for Kansas on her way back home, she asked my mother if she could keep me for the summer. I was three years old, very obedient, talked proper and more than anything else, I looked as if I could have been Mattie's son.

My mother initially squashed the idea, but then thought that maybe a break would be perfect while she adjusted to life in Memphis, so ultimately, she approved of the trip, but asked Mattie if she was also willing to take my brother.

Robin was deemed by doctors as mentally retarded, however, as he got older, we found out that Robin indeed had a lot of brains; more so than most people gave him credit for as well as a lot of common sense, but Mattie wanted no part of him.

Mattie wanted me because I was the model child, but mainly because she had no kids of her own. However, there was a specific reason behind why Mattie couldn't have kids.

My mother later explained to me how, when Mamie Echols found out Mattie was pregnant years prior, she took a coat hanger and shoved it up Mattie's vagina and into her birth canal, not only killing the fetus, but also ruining Mattie for life from ever being able have a child. I guess you can figure out that it was Mamie Echols who was the wicked witch I mentioned earlier; the one that we moved next door to. She also happened to be my great-grandmother.

Hmmm—Mamie Echols, it didn't even sound like a pleasant name. Who would name their daughter Mamie? She was an evil and wretched old lady who was despicable in every imaginary, or should I say un-imaginary way. She loved no one, cared about no one, not even herself.

She was a very miserable person and lived a miserable life and it seemed that her sole purpose of living was to make everyone around her unhappy. It actually sounds like someone else I currently know, but I don't dare mention their name. She never offered a kind word, gesture or act towards anyone and condemned anyone who tried to show kindness to her or anyone else. She was a ruthless person by all accounts. While my great-grandmother was busy making everyone else miserable, Mattie and I were on a plane and on our way Kansas.

ME DURING GOOD TIMES WHILE LIVING WITH AUNT MATTIE

During my stay in Kansas, Aunt Mattie spoiled me no end, buying me whatever I wanted. She took me to see the Kansas City Royals which was in their first year as an expansion team. We also went shopping all of the time, so I was always dressed in the best of clothes. She bought me my first tricycle and I also had a pet Chihuahua that I played with. I even had

A Father's Double Life

my very own room; yeah, I was living the life for a little while; however there was a saying,

"Nothing good lasts forever."

As the summer months zoomed by, we were well into mid-Autumn and my mother was getting closer to delivery. She wanted me back in Memphis to be part of my sister's birth. However, I wasn't missing the deplorable living conditions in which my parents were living and wanted to stay with Aunt Mattie. There would then be a struggle between my mother and Aunt, because Mattie tried to keep me for herself, but my mother finally got me back and just in time for my sister to be born, November 25th, 1969. Her name was Wendy.

After giving birth to my new sibling, we were all babysat next door in the adjoining duplex by none other than, Mamie Echols, the wicked witch, which meant when I described our house, I was describing hers as well.

Her home was cluttered, so much to the degree that it seemed as if she had saved everything she had ever been given over the entire seventy years of her life. There was hardly any room to walk and you had to weave your way through a maze of junk.

IN THIS 1972 PICTURE FROM LEFT TO RIGHT
IS MAMIE ECHOLS (THE WICKED WITCH), MY
GRANDFATHER JOHN AND AUNT MATTIE

Michael Cavicante

Let's not even talk about the roaches. Oh my goodness how the roaches had invaded her house. They were climbing up and down the walls, across the floors, on the ceilings, out of the faucet, over the dishes, and when I opened a drawer to get silverware, they practically handed me a utensil. I watched my great-grandmother swat and kill them with her bare hands; how revolting.

Standing five foot six inches, Mamie was light-skinned, wiry, and her face looked of worn leather. She also wore thin-rimmed, wire framed glasses and a hair net over her head. That's right; she not only acted like a witch, but also looked like one.

We were under her reign for two more years, until 1971. It was March and I had just turned five years old when Mamie Echols was babysitting my siblings and me. For the last couple of years, beans were all we had ever eaten, nothing different, nothing new, just beans.

Every Sunday, her routine was the same. She would go into the kitchen, clean a big, three-gallon pot, pour four or five packages of beans into it and then fill with water. She then brought the pot to a boil, while cutting onions, bacon, ham and other seasonings into it. After stirring and boiling for about thirty minutes, she would let the pot simmer for several hours and ultimately the legumes were ready to eat.

Navy Beans, Army Beans, Pinto Beans or Kidney Beans, take your choice, it really didn't matter; they were beans just the same. And they weren't just for dinner; we also ate them for breakfast and lunch. To say the least, there had to come a point and time where beans can't be wanted for any meal; forget three times a day.

That particular day eventually arrived for me, one March afternoon in 1971, when Mamie served up guess what? Yeah you got it—beans.

As I sat at a small table in the kitchen, a plate of beans sat there before me in a midst of an army of crawling roaches. I had actually gotten used to the roaches sadly enough. Okay maybe I'm fibbing just a bit; I could never get used to the roaches, but compared to the beans; those little, ugly, brown, contemptible, detestable little beans, just sickened me to my stomach. For me at that particular time, they were worse than any roach could ever be.

Before lifting my spoon, a nauseas feeling came over me and as my throat got tighter, I was choking before even taking my first bite.

I sat there thinking to myself as to how mean my great-grandmother was and wondering what would happen if I chose not to eat. What would

A Father's Double Life

she do? How would she react? I was left with very few options, and therefore, I knew that I had to eat that plate of beans.

As I slowly guided the spoon to my mouth, I had to close my eyes as just the look of them made me cringe. I opened my mouth and got bitter-beer face as I began to bite down. While removing the utensil from my lips and on the second bite, just as the first spoonful was about to hit the back of my throat, I regurgitated not only the beans, but also anything that was left in my digestive tract from the last several meals, which just so happened to be—beans.

With vomit all over me and in my plate, I sat there wondering what to do next. I felt her eerie presence around me when she approached my side,

"*What's wrong?*" in her crackling, old voice.

"*I just can't eat another bean, grandma. Do I have to eat them?*"

"*You will eat those damn beans or else!*"

I started crying and pleaded with her,

"*Please grandma, please don't make me eat any more beans.*"

I suddenly felt her cold, callused hands, which felt more like three-hundred grit sandpaper, grab me by the back of my neck and shove my face into the plate of yesterday's meal.

"*Eat those damn beans!*"

I struggled mightily and was able to break away from her talon-like grip. I lifted my head while crying as the conglomerate of bean juice and puke covered my innocent face.

I got up from the table and ran to the bathroom, knowing that she was about to somehow discipline me. She went outside and pulled a branch off of an old oak tree, stripped the leaves off of it, came into the bathroom and started to hit me with it.

She had me cornered between the bathtub and toilet while I sat on the floor covering my head. I felt the pain of that switch and as it lashed my skin, the pain got worse. I was screaming and crying when I got up and ran past her. She chased me through the little shack of a house and it wasn't the love shack either.

Being early March, it was still very cool outside, so there was a gas heater in operation in the middle room. While trying to escape her wrath, I tripped over a piece of that darned, torn linoleum and fell over the gas heater, only to burn my stomach. While smelling the melting of my burning flesh, I screamed at the top of my lungs and then seemingly went unconscious.

Michael Cavicante

When I awoke, my mother was putting salve on the burn that stretched at least eight inches across my stomach and navel. My mother soon thereafter, quit her job at Hyde Park laundry and stayed home with us full time. I thought to myself,

"If this was a taste of what the rest of my life would be like, then maybe I should jump back into my mother's womb and reverse this whole transaction."

But it was too late for that, for I was already born and very much alive."

It was plain to see that I wasn't in Kansas anymore.

Chapter 2
Life Goes On

You won't hear me talk a lot about Christmas in this story—mainly because we didn't have many Christmases to remember; I personally only remember maybe one or two. We seemingly always had a tree with lights every year, but I honestly don't remember anything special, aside from the fact that my mother read Bible Stories to us and explained the true meaning of what Christmas is all about. That was all well and good, but kids want presents and not reasons as to why we don't have them.

While growing up I was liked by most kids, but there were always bullies that picked on me for whatever reason. While living on Trigg, the bullies were Johnny and Damon, who were teenagers. They never laid a hand on me though. I think they just got a kick out of running me back into the house, which happened when I got a little older.

My brother, even though mentally handicapped, was accepted more than I was; why I don't know, but for whatever reason, he just fitted in better with the other kids. They knew he was mentally slow, so yeah, he was made fun of at times, but for the most part, kids had compassion for him. Even though a little slow, Robin did seem to have a lot more common sense than I did as a kid.

It was September, 1971, and time for me to start Kindergarten at Southside. I don't remember a lot about Kindergarten, except for the teacher making us lie down on mats and take naps. It seemed like that was all we ever did.

What I do recall as if it were yesterday was my mother making me wear a hot, itchy, short-sleeve, wool shirt to take school day pictures in May of 1972. I was absolutely miserable that day and it must have been a hundred degrees outside. I itched, scratched and was gloomy all day long as my picture on the front cover just might indicate.

Moving through the summer and into my first grade year, we enrolled at Cummings Elementary and would attend that school all the way through the third grade. The school was huge, standing three stories tall. It was just little over a mile away from home and we walked to and from school quite regularly. Being only eleven months apart, Robin and I for the most part, and throughout childhood, attended the same schools. He was one year ahead of me, but attended Special Education Classes.

On the way home, there was a milk factory on the corner of Bellevue and another cross street. We would see milk running from the factory and into the street, which we often had to step through. There was also a bank on the way where we occasionally stopped to get lollipops at the drive-thru teller window. My dad tried to be funny at times as he asked me one day, when I was much older,

"Why do banks have a drive thru?"
"I don't know dad, why?
"So the cars can meet their rightful owners."
I laughed loudly.
He tried to be funny, but it was few and far between.

After getting home from school, the line-up on television was, The Brady Bunch, Good Times, I adored Thelma by the way, and The Electric Company, which included Spider-Man. As a matter of fact, if they didn't show Spider-Man, I was thoroughly disappointed. It was the only reason I watched the show. The Beverly Hillbillies and Gilligan's Island topped out my favorites. I always thought that MaryAnn was a lot better looking than Ginger.

As the next several years went by and when not watching television, I made friends in the neighborhood with George, Jason and Roscoe. They lived directly across the street from us. They were a black family as there were no whites living on East Trigg; none that I could recall anyway. George was the eldest of the three boys, Jason was the middle and duh, Roscoe was the youngest. All were about two to three years apart. Their mother, Vanessa, was a thin albino woman and stood about five foot nine. Her and my mother would wind up being friends for the next thirty years.

A Father's Double Life

CUMMINGS ELEMENTARY SCHOOL

Right next door to them lived Yvette and her three sons, who happened to be Rollie, Kurt, and Mickey. Even though I was young, I was old enough to know that Yvette was an absolute fox. She was of light complexion and had this long, black, silky looking hair. She was absolutely the bomb-diggity.

With the eight of us living in such close proximity to each other, we boys often played hide and go-seek in the narrow streets, which was just wide enough for two cars to pass. It was really the only outdoor activity for us to do. I even remember what the seeker said while closing his eyes and leaning up against a telephone poll, while the rest of us went hiding,

"Last night, night before, twenty-four robbers at my door, mom went and let one in, hit 'em upside the head with the rolling pin, my mother told me to pick this one right over here."

And then the seeker would go look for us. It was pretty fun I guess, but it's not like there were a whole lot of places to hide.

Other than playing Hide and Go-Seek, my dad brought us kites homes to fly every fall, but they would only last for about a day or two because they usually got caught up in the trees and ruined. I also remember getting the t-shirts with the orange smiley faces which were a hot commodity back then. My dad tried to make us happy while they struggled to make ends meet.

Believe it or not, the main highlight while living on Trigg was seeing the Goodyear Blimp. Robin and I would be in the house and knew that it was nearby, because we heard the loud, resonant noise that it made and then ran outside to see it. It was huge and flew so close to the house that we could see people in the cockpit. It hovered around for a while seemingly circling the neighborhood, but then left our sight, at which time we became sad. It was docked at a nearby Goodyear Tire Store.

The other highlight was seeing our Grandfather. John was my mother's father and in his sixties. Sadly enough, he was Mamie's son and lived with her. It was plain to see that he was a momma's boy, and oh how she controlled him, manipulated him and eventually ruined him. He periodically sat on the wooden, bench-type swing, which hung by chain-like metal on their front porch. At times, I would go sit with him and listen as he talked about voodoo and witchcraft.

He had a paranoia that people were out to get him and talked in circles, not really making much sense at times. Even though I was young, I knew that my grandfather wasn't right, but I loved him very much; he was a sweet man. I blamed Mamie for him being the way that he was. Nonetheless, I listened to him while he rambled on, because I thought it would be rude to just get up and walk away. After he finished, he would reach into his pocket and give me any loose change that he had, and then off to the Sundry I went to buy candy. Lemonheads, Boston Baked Beans, Pixy-Stix, and Now & Laters were the hot items back then.

There were two Sundries, both located on the corner of Wilson and Gleason, but across the street from each other. I could always count on grandfather to give me his loose change.

My grandfather also had super-human strength. There was an old, black, 1954 Packard parked in their front yard. The car sat there forever, never moving, while having four flat tires. It had to be to impress us kids, because one day, he grabbed the back of the car and lifted it off the ground; no joking. There might have been a quarter inch clearance, but just the fact that he was able to lift it at all was amazing in itself. We thought he was Superman while we looked in astonishment, because afterwards, four or five of us tried to lift the car, but to no avail, it didn't budge.

While demonstrating his Atlas-like strength, Mamie came to the door and yelled at my grandfather.

"John, get your ass in this house and get ready for supper," poking her wretched face from behind the screen door.

I had to assume that they were eating beans; that's all she knew how to cook it seemed.

"Yes ma'm, I'm coming," my grandfather replied.

A Father's Double Life

"*Get in this house now!!*" As he shuffled quickly up the steps and into the front door

"*What an evil person,*" I thought to myself, while turning my head away from her with a scowl on my face. It was so sad to witness her control of him.

Times spent inside my house were spent listening to my parents' music. I was raised on such artists as Jim Croce, Billie Holliday, Bill Withers, Simon & Garfunkel, The Mamas and The Papas, The Carpenters, Carly Simon, CCR, and the Doobie Brothers, just to name a few. Oh yeah, how could I forget about Elvis Presley? We lived in Memphis for Pete's sake. Elvis was my favorite musician in the seventies with songs such as Suspicious Minds and Hound Dog; both are songs that I sing on Karaoke night to this very day.

I do remember playing with my Etch-A-Sketch and Rock'em-Sock'em Robots and we had some Tonka Toys as well. I learned after growing up, that no matter how short of money parents are, most will find a way to do for their kids and my parents did. Yes we struggled, but they did try.

I never knew where it came from, but there was a white clown suit that had red polka dots on it. I would routinely put it on, paint my nose and cheeks red while using my mother's lipstick, and afterwards, went around the neighborhood trying to make people laugh. I guess I was craving attention, because my baby sister was getting all of it from my parents, so there was a little resentment there.

My mother explained that I didn't have enough time to be the baby, because I was only three when Wendy was born. Well now that I am older, I can only imagine how my brother felt, because I came along just eleven months after him. I do remember trying to do anything to get my father's attention, but he was always so wrapped up into Wendy that I was always second to her, or that's the way it seemed anyway.

On Sundays, I would watch other neighborhood kids go to church and wanted to go badly. They had on their shirts, ties, and shiny shoes. I asked, if not begged my mother at times if I could go to church, but she would tell me "*No.*" She thought our clothes were too shoddy to be attending services. My mother bought our clothes from a Goodwill Store, not far away on Bellevue Avenue. We wore polyester pants most of the time because she got them for like two dollars a pair.

Outside of wanting to go to church, we did mischievous things as most young boys do, or maybe I should say that I did mischievous things.

My third grade year was over and in the early summer of 1975 my brother and I were at Bellevue Park, which was the city park right up the road from where we lived. It had the greenest grass I had ever seen, a couple of swing sets, a merry-go round, a sandbox, slides, monkey bars and a jungle gym.

It was a beautiful day and we had just finished playing on the swings. I suggested to Robin that we walk to the boulevard and look at the bustling traffic, so we did, while walking another fifty yards or so.

After arriving at the sidewalk that ran along Bellevue Avenue, I could smell the aroma of freshly, cooked, fried chicken coming from Jack Pirtle's, which was adjacent to the park; Mmmm—it sure smelled good. We stood there and watched automobiles, big eighteen wheelers roar by, which also included the trucks pulling out of the Roadway Trucking Company, located next to the park. It was so exciting.

As my eyes continued to scan the surroundings, I looked up and spotted a red box on a utility pole that we were standing next to. It read, "Fire Alarm". I became curious.

"Robin, let's pull the Fire alarm to see what will happen."

"No! If you do, I'm leaving!"

I must say that I manipulated him a lot. I knew that he was the eldest, but I also knew that it was him who looked up to me. Well you know what happened next. That's right, I pulled the lever and like a couple of idiots, we stood there to see what would happen.

Within minutes, we heard sirens and a roaring engine. We saw a Firetruck as it approached us heading south, with red lights flashing and horn blowing. I guess I thought they were going to pass right by us, and they did while on the other side of the street.

We stood there and watched while the truck went up the street towards the South Parkway intersection, made a u-turn, only to come back to the exact point where we were standing. It was the most astonishing thing I had ever seen.

I stood there in awe with my mouth wide open and speechless, when a giant figure of a man, the Fire Chief, got out of a candy-apple red fire car and approached us. His body soon eclipsed the sun and it got dark all of a sudden. I stood there while not saying a word and in a state of trance, while looking up at the hulking man. He looked down at us and said,

"Did you kids pull this fire alarm?" while pointing at it.

After taking a sizable swallow, I replied

"Yes Sir."

"This is not a toy. You shouldn't have done it."

A Father's Double Life

I felt very remorseful and started crying.

"Are we in trouble Sir?" while rubbing my eyes.

"No, but we need to get you kids home." He placed his hand gently on my shoulder.

"Do you want to ride in my shiny red car?"

My face brightened up immediately and the tears quickly subsided.

"Sure, can you sound the siren?" I asked, as he led us to the car.

"No, we're not going to do that," he replied, with a slight smirk on his face.

After we were guided into the car, I gave him directions to our home and it took all of only two minutes to get there. After arriving at our house, the Fire Chief escorted us to the front door and knocked. After my mother answered, the Fire Chief responded,

"Are these your kids ma'm?"

"Why yes they are. Are they okay?"

"They are just fine ma'm., they just pulled down the Fire Alarm on Bellevue and we responded only to find your kids standing right next to it."

"They aren't in any trouble are they?"

"No ma'm, I just wanted to make sure they got home safely."

"Why thank you very much Sir."

"You're very welcome Ma'm." The Fire Chief then turned and walked away while my mother opened the door to let us in.

"Mom, we got to ride in the Red Car!" I exclaimed as if nothing was wrong.

But after she closed that door, I all of a sudden knew that everything was wrong.

For the first time ever, I witnessed my mother in a rage, when she grabbed a belt and chased me under the bed. My joy from riding in that shiny, red car quickly turned to fear. My mother knew that I was the ringleader of everything that happened, both good and bad.

While underneath the bed, I saw her feet pace the floor.

"Come from under that bed!"

"I'm sorry mom."

"How dare you embarrass me like that?"

"I'm sorry mom." as my tears started up again.

I was sure that she couldn't get to me and felt pretty safe, but I was wrong. She took the end of a broomstick handle and shoved it under the bed at me, while poking me in the stomach a couple of times while she swore.

"*Darn you, you better never embarrass me like that again!*" as she continued to poke

"*I'm sorry mommy, I'm sorry.*" as I tried to grab the handle but she eventually gave up.

I had never seen my mother so angry.

I guess my dad was on the road or something, because he wasn't home and we went to bed that night without any more incidents.

Hours later, around two in the morning and while sleeping, we were both suddenly awakened with a belt across our backsides. I opened my eyes and saw my father in a fit of rage, wailing away at both of us.

Can you imagine how startled and terrified we were being awakened in the middle of the night with a belt? I yelled, screamed and cried while trying to protect myself with the covers, but he pulled them away from me and caught my bare skin. He also talked while beating us.

"*So you're going to give your mother a hard time while I'm gone, huh?*"

"*I'm sorry, daddy, I'm sorry.*" I screamed at the top of my lungs.

I thought I was in hell, probably because he looked like the devil. His hair stood up on top of his head to resemble horns and his eyes were that of man with no soul. He struck us with that thick, leather belt, while hitting us with almost every stroke. I'm sure he killed a roach or two as well, because I saw several dead ones on the floor when my dad was done. He talked to us some more while wailing away.

"*You better behave yourselves while I'm gone, you hear me?*"

"*Yes daddy, I will daddy,*" were words also echoed by my brother.

The massacre would have probably continued for a lot longer if my mother hadn't come in the room and stopped my madman of a father.

His messages was heard loud and clear as it was a long, long time before I got another beating. The incident left unsightly welts on me as I bruised very easily, being of light complexion. They were on my arms, legs, and torso. Just about everywhere the belt landed, there was a bruise.

At the tender age of nine, my father had put the fear of God in me. It was also at that precise point in my life, when I said to myself,

"*My daddy is crazy.*"

We knew if we acted up, we would pay for it with some skin off of our rear ends. Sometimes my father went to extremes though, hitting us with whatever was in his arms reach. I said that would be my last beating for a while, but it didn't mean that he wouldn't pick up things and hit us with them. It could have been an extension cord, a fly swatter (how nasty), an umbrella, or just about anything that could inflict enough pain to get our attention.

Not long after the East Trigg bludgeoning, my dad bought Robin and I some skates. I guess he realized that we were bored and had nothing better to do than to go around pulling down fire alarms. We learned how to skate, but our knees paid the price, because we fell all of the time and came home with bloodied legs quite often.

There was a church parking lot right around the corner that had just gotten paved. The surface was as smooth as a baby's bottom and ideal for skating. Robin and I went there and skated for hours on end, and afterwards, raced home; I usually always won. Robin followed me wherever I went as he loved me and I loved him.

As the summer of 1975 slowly faded away, my dad came home with news that he had gotten a great trucking job with Gordon's Transport. Of course, I was too young to know what a great job was, but I did know that in no time we were gone and moving to Whitehaven, which at the time, was a very nice part of Memphis.

The job was so good that my father took Robin and me with him one day to pick up his weekly check. However when we got there, my father asked us to keep our heads down until we left, so Robin and I ducked down in the back seat until my dad was back in the car and drove off. I didn't understand why he had done that, but I told my mother about it when we got home and the reason became apparent as I heard my mother arguing with my father in the other room.

"Are you embarrassed of your own kids?"

"No."

"Then why did you have them duck down in the back seat?"

"Because we're in the south now and ninety-nine percent of the truckers at Gordon's are white and prejudiced, so if they saw the kids, I might lose my job."

"If that's the way you felt, then why did you take them with you?"

"Because I didn't think about it until I got there."

"If you can't expose your kids to your own co-workers, then you don't need to work there."

"But we need the money."

"I don't give a damn about the money, these are your kids!"

"Aw shut the hell up woman!" as the argument ended.

As I listened, I cried to myself. Robin was also smart enough to understand and with him being much darker, I can only imagine how he felt.

Our own father was ashamed of us. It wasn't a good feeling and I think from that day on, my brother resented being dark-skinned, because throughout my childhood he made comments that he hated himself and wished he were me.

Over the years, we listened while my father talked about his white trucker buddies and life on the road, but never would we ever have the pleasure of being introduced to any of his so-called friends.

By the way he talked, his fellow truckers thought the world of him. He had personality, charisma, looks, and could charm the skin right off a snake, but with everything going for him, he denied his own kids. I don't recall him even carrying pictures of us, now that I think about it. It seems like the more I write, the more I realize how he really was.

While at home, he did play around with us and showed obvious love, but he just wasn't going to be seen with us while in the company of his associates. I use that word because if they were really his friends, than they wouldn't care about our darker skin color and lack of straight hair. I guess this was just the start of what would be a gradual unveiling of my father's character as the years went by.

In the mean time, with dear old dad now making more money, we were in the process of moving and getting out of the roach motel. There wasn't a whole lot to move; mostly just clothes if you want to call them that. I like to refer to them as rags. My only wish was that we left the roaches and rats behind.

A Father's Double Life

MY FATHER STANDS NEXT TO HIS EIGHTEEN-WHEELER
PRIOR TO GETTING THE JOB AT GORDON'S

Chapter 3
Having Faith

It was late summer, 1975. I was nine years old and after a couple of horrific incidents, I was unsure of what to expect next as all types of thoughts were going through my head.

"Was this the way a human being is supposed to live? Was I never allowed to make any mistakes without getting awakened in the middle of the night with a strap across my backside? Were roaches and beatings what life was all about? Why was dad never home, and when he was, why didn't he spend any time with us? Why were people different colors and why did people hate others just by the color of their skin? How was mom able to take her hair off of her head and lay it anywhere in the house, but always made sure to put her hair back on when someone knocked on the door? I tried to remove my hair many times as a kid, but was never able to achieve what I saw my mother do countless times. What was that squeaking sound, along with the knocks on the wall coming from my parent's room late at night, and why was she moaning? I wanted answers to these questions and more, but never asked why."

I guess that would be part of who I was throughout my childhood. I always wondered why, but never asked any questions. For the most part, I was left to figure out things on my own. A lot of things of course, I never did figure out, but just dealt with.

My way of dealing with everything was just to keep it bottled up inside, no matter what happened to blindside me and to just move on with life. It's called resiliency, and resiliency is what I would have to have if I was going to make it in this world.

While I was pondering those thoughts, we were busy moving into our house on Faith Cove. I guess Faith Cove was the appropriate name for the street, because my mother would have to have faith that we would be able to pay the rent.

Situated in a cul-de-sac, the house was an all brick, ranch style home. It had three bedrooms, a kitchen, dining room and living room. The backyard was enclosed with a six-foot tall, wooden, privacy fence.

There was little to no furniture inside the house and we had outgrown the small beds we slept in while living on Trigg, so we slept on mattresses placed on the floor, which had no carpet, just tile. I could only dream of what it would have been like to have real carpeted floors. We only had one television in the house which was a small, thirteen-inch model that sat on a small table in the kitchen.

During our stay on Faith Cove and to my delight, I never saw a roach. That alone was a bonus for me. I started school at Fairley Elementary for my fourth grade year in the fall of 1975.

My teacher was Ms. Gaither and I will never forget her as she was officially, my very first, childhood crush. She was a young, white lady with blonde hair and extremely attractive. She reminded me of Sally Struthers from "All in the Family" fame. It was a hit television show around that time.

Because of my new teacher, I looked forward to going to school every day and was exceptionally bright, so I breezed through my elementary years.

I loved school anyway, but Ms. Gaither made time in class more of a joy. There were times when I would be sitting at my desk mesmerized by her beauty while she wrote on the chalkboard. I had my elbow on the desk, cheek resting in hand and stared at her as she glided across the room. I watched her lips moving while she talked, but didn't hear a word she was saying. I was definitely in la-la land.

I was in such a daze from her beauty at times that I had to be nudged by fellow students in order get my attention, at which point my head fell off of my hand and almost hit the desk as if I were being awakened.

One day after school, I was still daydreaming of Ms. Gaither while walking home when I noticed a black kid following me. I soon came out of my daze and began to walk faster, but his pace also quickened. I eventually started running and he did the same. I made it all the way to my front yard when the boy caught me, wrestled me to the ground, sat on me and beat my face in with brass knuckles for no apparent reason.

My mother obviously heard my screaming when she came outside and got the boy off me as he then ran away. My mother helped me into the house with my face all bloodied. She would lick my wounds (not literally), clean me up and hold me in her arms like a baby while I cried.

"Why do kids pick on me?"
"They are just jealous of your cute looks."
"Am I really cute?"
"You are not only cute, you are very handsome." She pulled me closer and smothered my face against her chest.

I wasn't so handsome when going to school the next day. My face was swollen and bruised while kids asked me what had happened. Of course I told them that I had gotten beaten up. The wounds healed and I would of course be okay, but pain whether it was mental or physical, self-inflicted or not, would be part of my life for years to come, so that was just the beginning.

Speaking of pain, several months had gone by when one day, my mother was smoking a cigarette as she did from time to time. I hated seeing her smoke and also hated the smell. It gagged me every time she lit up. I was pretty bright, but remember little common sense at the time. I did know that smoking was hazardous to your health.

My dad also smoked. I still remember those Pall Mall Cigarettes that came in a red pack and had no filters, but I knew that there was little hope for him. Either that or I was just too afraid to tell him to quit. I would say that the latter was the reason more so than the first.

One day, while my mother sat at the kitchen table smoking, I sat across from her. I watched her put that cigarette up to her lips and take a drag. I noticed how the end of it got brighter while taking that drag. She looked so relaxed while exhaling. It seemed that smoking gave her much pleasure.

Well, with all of my brightness, I took two fingers and extinguished that cigarette by pinching the end. It hurt like the dickens, but I tried to play it off while telling my mother that I was going to do that every time she lit up while at the same time waving my hand in pain.

"What the heck are you doing?" she yelled.
"I'm sorry mommy; I just hate seeing you smoke."
"That was a stupid thing to do! What were you thinking?"
"I didn't know it was going to be that hot. I'm sorry."

She was mad at me for doing such a foolish thing, but I guess she realized that I did it because I loved her. She then grabbed and hugged me.

"I'm sorry for yelling at you sweetheart. I love you so much." She kissed me on the forehead.

She pulled me back and looked me in the eyes.
"You want mommy to quit smoking?"
"Yes mommy, more than anything in this whole world."
"Why?"
"Because smoking is bad for you and I don't want anything to happen to you."

She pulled me back close to her and while rocking me, she replied,
"Okay son, if you want mommy to quit, mommy will quit."
"Today, mommy?"
"Yes honey, today."

I wrapped my arms around her and squeezed her tightly while relishing the moment.

My mother quit smoking for good that very day. I personally suffered from minor burns for a couple of weeks on my two fingers, but it was worth it if it meant that she wasn't going to smoke anymore.

Outside of doing silly little things, mostly to my own detriment, I didn't ask for a lot as a kid but I was unhappy because my dad had brought home a couple of records. What was significant about those records was that they had my brother and sister's names in them.

One of the songs was *"Fly Robin Fly"* by the Silver Convention. The song had previously been a number one hit on the soul singles chart and I really liked it. The other song was *"Windy"* by the Association, which had also been a number one hit on Billboard's Hot 100 back in July of 1967. I was far from being a brat, but I whined to my mother.

"Why do Robin and Wendy both have songs mommy?"
"There just songs honey, that's all they are."
"Well I want a song too." I said, as I poked my bottom lip out.
"We will see what we can do about that, okay?"

It may have seemed trivial, but it made me very unhappy and I moped around for several days.

Within a week, my father came home with a record for me, and it was, *"Michael Row the Boat Ashore"*. It was recorded by several artists and was originally an African-American Spiritual during the civil war, so the song had a long history.

Of course at that point in time, I didn't know the history of the song, nor did I care. All I did know was that I was elated and overjoyed that I now had my own song. A smile stretched on my face from ear to ear as it played.

"How do you like it baby?"

"It is the greatest song that I have ever heard mommy. Thank you so much." I hugged her.
"Thank daddy, he brought it home for you."
I ran over to my father and gave him a hug, which he reciprocated.
"Thanks daddy."
"You're welcome, Mike the Tike," which was his new nickname for me.

As the song played, I danced with joy as my parents beamed. My mother started singing along with her angelic voice while also dancing with me.

The Highwaymen recorded the song in 1961. It hit number one on the Billboard Hot 100 and stayed there for two weeks in September of that year and also topped the UK charts while peaking at number one, just a month later, October twelfth, 1961. The version we were listening to belonged to Peter, Paul and Mary.

It seemed that any song with a name in it was destined to be a number one hit, or was it because they had our names in those particular songs? Whatever the reason, I think it was amazing that all three of these songs, at one time or another, were all number one hits.

I don't remember asking for much as a kid, nor was I hard kid to please or make happy. I just wanted a song with my name in the title because Robin and Wendy had one.

As far as friends, I only had one who lived several blocks away on Spindlewood, which was across Neely Road; his name was Steve. The only thing I remember about him was being invited to his home during the Christmas Holidays. He lived in this really nice two-story house.

When I got over there, I was in awe; I mean he had everything. The house was decorated with holly and mistletoe. There were Christmas lights strung over the balcony of the staircase and mantle; there were stockings hanging from the fireplace, not to mention the biggest Christmas tree I had ever seen. There was a toy train going around the tree. The smell of cookies and cakes being baked was in the air, lights flickering, Christmas music playing and gift wrapped presents everywhere. I was totally amazed by what I was witnessing.

"What a lucky kid." I thought to myself.

I had never wished to be anybody, nor was I ever the jealous type, but I had wished that I could some day, be part of a Christmas like Steve was obviously accustomed to having.

"Would I ever experience a Christmas like that?" I wondered.

Michael Cavicante

    As I continued to be amazed by Steve's blessings, we played games, enjoyed Egg Nog and watched Television. I had never had Egg Nog before; boy was that some good stuff. I guess you can understand why I remembered that moment in time.

    After spending the night at Steve's House, I returned to my humdrum existence of a home on Faith Cove. How could any kid witness and experience what I had just experienced while spending time with Steve and be enthused about returning to my surroundings? The answer was simple, I wasn't, but nonetheless, never really complained or talked about what I wished I had. I was smart enough to know that the possibilities of it ever happening was probably nil, so I just dealt with it.

    Those were the main events that took place on Faith Cove as I found out that faith doesn't always prevail. My parents were unable to pay the rent and we found ourselves moving again from what would be the nicest house that my siblings and I would live in as children, within only a year and in the summer of 1976. After receiving an eviction notice, my parents found what would be the home where we would live until I was nineteen years old.

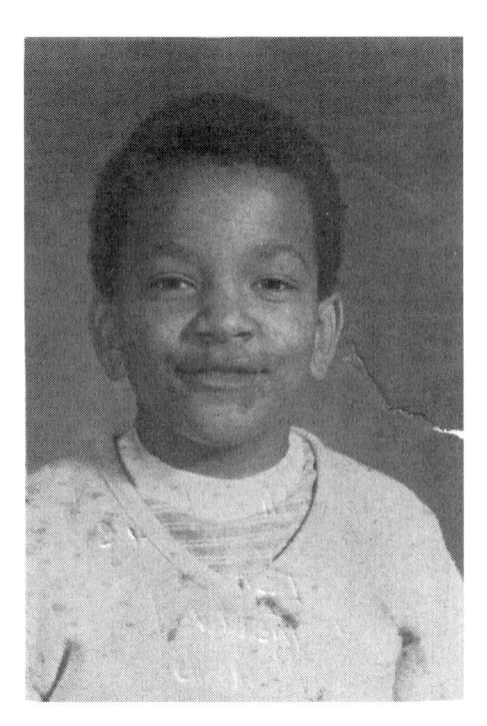

ME AT TEN YEARS OLD AND COULD POSSIBLY BE THE LAST SMILE SEEN ON MY FACE FOR A VERY LONG TIME

A Father's Double Life

At ten years old, I was growing and maturing at a rapid pace. You probably wouldn't be able to tell by the song incident, but fact is, I had already been through a lot. Yep, at an early age, I was becoming a man as my childhood so far had been anything but what a childhood should be. I guess I am speaking for my siblings as well, but the upcoming years were the worst to come, for me especially.

I was a stocky kid for my age and I guess I can thank my great-grandmother for that, with all of the beans that she fed me. I remember weighing myself for the very first time at the age of ten; I was a whopping one hundred sixty pounds. In contrast, at the time this book was published, my son was fourteen and weighed one hundred seventy pounds and he was pretty hefty.

With that being said, I was certainly big and strong enough to help the family load up the car. With mattresses tied down on the roof, my brother and I held them down while our arms stuck out of the window from the back seat. My dad drove slowly so they wouldn't fly off. Our new car was a shiny, red 1974 Pontiac Bonneville; the same color as that Fire Department Car.

We arrived at our home on West Ball Road in Prospect Park that summer. The neighborhood was secluded off of the main streets and very shaded with a lot of trees; shucks, nineteen pine trees in our front yard alone.

Maybe that was why it was called Prospect Park, because it probably was a city park before they built the homes. I really don't know, just wondering. The neighborhood had four main roads in the neighborhood that all ran parallel to each other and they were, Ball, Rutgers, Colgate and Alcy, with two side streets intersecting all four.

Even though the neighborhood was breathtakingly beautiful, our new house needed a lot of work and was made of stucco. Inside, the walls were white, but a dingy white, as if they hadn't been painted in years. It had an upstairs with two bedrooms which is where Robin and I would sleep. The rooms were conjoined with no door separating the two; so really, it was just one big room. I could lie in my bed and see my brother only ten feet away lying in his.

The downstairs consisted of two separate bedrooms side by side that took up the rear of the house which my parents and sister occupied. Both bedrooms shared one common closet with doors on opposite ends. This was a very significant feature of the house and you will find out later as to why.

A living room and dining room occupied the front of the house, with the kitchen being right off of the dining room and a bathroom would complete the dwelling. Oh yeah; the house did have a wood burning fireplace. Maybe someone should have told my dad that it was wood that was supposed to be burned.

The walls upstairs were paper-thin. You could put a hole through them if you leaned on them hard enough and there was no insulation between the inner and outer walls. Needless to say, it was very hot in the summer and extremely cold in the winter. The one air conditioning unit in the house was placed in the dining room window, but didn't have enough BTU's to cool the whole house, only that particular room.

During the summer months, my father put up sheets at the two doorways entering the dining room, so if you wanted some comfort you could go sit in there. If you're wondering why there wasn't and air conditioning unit placed in the living room, there wasn't a window in the living room that would accommodate a unit. Oh yeah, you can also bet that there was an air conditioning unit in my father's bedroom. My dad wasn't about to be uncomfortable while he slept; that wasn't going to happen.

In the winter months it was the same situation, but the sheets instead covered the kitchen doorways, because the stove is what warmed the kitchen and that part of the house, and therefore, was the room we went to when we wanted to get warm. The upstairs was cooled with fans in the summer, no a/c units for us, and in the winter, we covered up with a lot of blankets as any heat produced escaped right through the dry wall.

Our landlord's name was Clinton. He was a white, good-looking man resembling Tom Selleck of Magnum P.I. As would have it, he was a Memphis Police Officer and I think my mother had a little crush on him. She always made sure that she looked her best when he came by to collect the rent, which was $225/mth; remember this was 1976, okay?

All in all and considering the home's poor condition, it was a far cry from the four room, rat and roach-infested, shot-gun house on Trigg, but still wasn't as nice as our home on Faith Cove, but I guess we could consider ourselves blessed to be out of that situation and at least living in a much nicer neighborhood than that of the one on Trigg.

Chapter 4
Nine lives going fast

As the summer progressed, I made a new friend, but how we met was unconventional. I pulled out of our driveway on my bicycle one day and was hit by a car. The car barely tapped me, thanks to the driver stopping very quickly, but still hit the bike just enough to knock me over. I lay there on the street when a tall, young, black kid got out of the car. I thought he was going to beat me up because that was what I had become accustomed to.

"Are you okay man?" he asked, as he helped me to my feet.
"Yes; I am okay."
"You talk kind of funny, where are you from?"
"California."
"Are you new to the neighborhood?"
"Yes sir."
"Sir? He then laughs, *"My name is Chris. What's your name?"*
"Michael."
"Well Michael, you got to look both ways before pulling out that driveway the way you did. If I had been going fast, this wouldn't have been pretty, so be careful."
"Yes sir."
"It's Chris."
"Okay."
"Do you play basketball? He asked.
"No, I have never played before."

"Well, I live on top of the hill on Rutgers. If you want to come play, you can, okay?"
"Okay sir."
"Mike, its Chris."
"Okay Chris."

I accepted the invitation to play basketball, but it wasn't Chris who would become my friend, it was Willie, his brother. Willie was a thin, brown-skinned boy and a couple of years older than me, but we had a great time together and played basketball daily. Until I moved to Ball Road, I had never played basketball, or football for that matter which we also played often. Willie was funny and always kept me laughing, which was a good prescription for some of the pain that I would endure over the years to come.

Willie also had a sister named Jackie. She had big, pretty eyes that just jumped out at you and wore the tightest jeans; she was fine. Always very pleasant and nice to me over the years, Jackie and I never really engaged in any lengthy dialogue. For the most part it was always just a hello and good-bye.

That summer, I also learned how to swim, but didn't learn by taking lessons. Do you remember Vanessa? No, not the fox, but the other one, the albino woman. Well one day, she took Robin and me, along with her three sons to a public swimming pool at Fuller State Park, which was absolutely gorgeous.

As you entered, it looked like an enchanted forest of some kind. There were tall trees everywhere and the road entering the playground was long, winding and narrow. While driving deeper into the park, I could see the pool nestled back in the woods. I couldn't believe that something so nice was practically free. It only cost twenty-five cents to get in.

One particular summer day, it seemed like every kid in Memphis was at the pool, while it had been our fourth or fifth trip there. Robin and I stayed at the shallow end of the pool because we didn't know how to swim.

Wanting to take a break, I got out of the water to walk around a bit. While strolling near the deep end, which was twelve feet, I was pushed into the water. I was so scared while wondering what had just happened, but there was no time for panicking as I sunk straight to the bottom. After feeling my feet touch the pool bottom, I used my powerful legs to push myself back to the surface.

"*Help help!*" as I flailed away.

But no one responded and I sunk back to the bottom, and again, pushed my way back to the surface with my head barely getting above water.

"Help help!"

But not one person came to my rescue. All of a sudden, I started stroking my arms and feet while struggling mightily to stay afloat.

Flailing away, I miraculously made it to the wall and held on while coughing up water and breathing heavily. After catching my breath, I pulled myself up and onto the side of the pool. I lay there on my back wondering who had pushed me in while the hot sun baked my skin. After several minutes, I realized that I had swum to the edge of the pool. Had I learned how to swim?

After regaining my wits, I got up, walked around while asking several kids who had pushed me in, but nobody would tell me. After failing to find out who the culprit was, I jumped back into the shallow end of the pool to test out my technique, and surely, I had learned how to swim. It wasn't long before I was doing somersaults off the diving board at the deep end of the pool, that very same day.

The somersaults would end several visits later after hitting back-first while jumping off of the high diving board. It stung so badly that it felt like I had hit a brick wall. I would never again do another somersault off a diving board.

Roscoe, Vanessa's son, later confessed to pushing me in and apologized to me and I accepted. I was mad at what he had done, because I could have very well lost my life on that day, but I had always been very forgiving and therefore accepted his apology. I also realized that if he hadn't pushed me in, I probably would have never learned how to swim which was an ability I would need later in life. My mother had always told me that everything happened for a reason.

As the summer of 1976 came to an end, it was time to start my fifth grade year at Willow Oaks Elementary and we were bussed for the very first time.

Willow Oaks was a nice school. It was a one level brick building, but its boundaries were broad and wide. There was a main corridor that ran parallel with the main road and at least four hallways that branched off of it separately while leading back to the street, with doors at the ends, which is where we entered the building en route to our classes.

The big, yellow, school busses lined up at least eight in a row on the street for drop-off and pick-up. The school was situated in a very nice and quiet, middle-class neighborhood.

In the morning, after we got dressed for school, it was customary to eat a bowl of Corn Flakes which was our new breakfast food; it was the highlight of our morning. I remember the big, white box with the rooster on the front that had the colored comb on top of his head.

We sat at the kitchen table while my mother poured them in a big bowl and at times, cut bananas into the cereal. Do you recall the big bowl that Jethro ate out of on the Beverly Hillbillies? Well the bowl that we ate out of resembled that one.

Robin always ate like he had never eaten before, devouring his food in no time at all. His favorite thing to do was reading the cereal box while consuming his meal. I don't know how much material was on that Corn Flake box, but everyday, he sat at the table with the box in front of him and read it.

After breakfast, Robin and I headed to the bus stop. On days that it rained, the insides of my shoes got soaked, thanks largely in part to the holes at the bottom. My mother put cardboard inside to help keep the water out when it rained. The cardboard she used was from those empty Corn Flake boxes, she would tell me,

"Now I'm going to fold this cardboard and put it in the bottom of your shoes so your feet won't get wet."

Well guess what? It didn't work. My socks were soaked before I even made it to the bus stop. I would get to school, into the building and my shoes squeaked loudly. You could hear the squishing sound of the water inside when my feet struck the floor.

After making it to class, I sat at my desk wiggling my toes, because the soaked socks were very uncomfortable. Even by the end of the school day eight hours later, my socks were still damp. I would finally get home and take them off with my feet all moist and pasty. I used my hands to get the moisture off and then of course, washed my hands.

After washing my hands, peanut butter and jelly sandwiches were the norm for our after school meal, and more often than not, was our final meal of the day. I looked forward to them though as my mother served us two or three sandwiches at times along with a big glass of milk.

The remainder of the year went uneventful and we roared passed the holidays and into 1977. The year started with the thirty-ninth President of the United States being inaugurated on January 20th, and his name was Jimmy Carter. He had previously served as Governor of Georgia.

While Jimmy and his wife, First Lady Rosalyn, were getting acclimated to life in the White House, my fifth grade year went on and ended uneventfully while moving into the summer.

The movie of that decade so far, had been JAWS, which had been released two years prior, in 1975. We had never been to a movie before, but that was about to change with the release of Star Wars. The movie received so much hype and was talked about so much amongst my peers, that there was no way that my parents weren't going to take us to see it.

So one early summer night, Robin, Wendy, and myself, were treated to what would be our first flick to be seen in a theatre. We were so excited and the movie didn't disappoint as new technology, laser beams, and the galaxy mesmerized us. That summer, *"Star Wars"* became the highest grossing movie release ever, and took in a whopping $460million at the box office. It would remain in the number one spot for a staggering twenty years.

It was also the same summer that my siblings and I were introduced to pancakes for the very first time.

I woke up one morning and the aroma of something different was in the air. I got out of the bed, put on my robe and my nose led me to the kitchen. I saw my mother flipping something, so I walked over to the stove.

"Good morning mom."
"Good morning my beautiful son."
"What are you cooking?"
"Pancakes."

I watched her stand over the stove and flip them, while they became a golden brown. She took them out of the sizzling skillet, piled them on a plate and while I looked in astonishment, she stacked them four or five high. She then spread butter on them and poured maple syrup over the mountain of steamy, fluffy flapjacks while my mouth watered. I grabbed a fork and with utensil in hand, I was ready to dig in while sitting at the table.

I then watched her lift the plate and with my eyes getting as big as those pancakes, I salivated while licking my chops like a dog. I was about to have my first serving of flapjacks. I waited in anticipation while she walked towards me, but continued right past me, out of the kitchen and into the living room where my father was sitting as I got up to follow her.

I suddenly stopped and peeked around the corner as she sat the plate in front of my dad. I said good morning to my father and he just mumbled. I sadly returned to the kitchen and had to wait my turn.

Minutes later, Robin came downstairs.
"What are you cooking Mom?"
"Pancakes."

Soon, we were both sitting at the table with forks in hand waiting for our pancakes. You would have thought we hadn't eaten in days. It seemed like it took forever for us to get served, but when we did, Oh My Gosh!! It was the best thing I had ever tasted. I think my mom had given us three apiece. Well we wanted more.

We must have eaten seven or eight pancakes each that morning. As you can probably tell, my mother never taught us portion control. Give 'em as much as they can eat was her philosophy. For that reason, all of us, with the exception of Robin who was blessed with a super metabolism, struggled with our weight.

Pancakes were cheap to make and filling, so the added fact that we loved them made them an easy choice for her. We were served pancakes often for breakfast during the summer months and on weekends during school months.

Robin literally licked the plate to make sure he consumed any remaining syrup. He would lift the plate to his mouth and tilt it at a forty-five degree angle while licking every drop of molasses. Shucks—he licked the plate so clean, that if we hadn't seen him do it, my mother could have put the plate back on the shelf for use and we wouldn't have known the difference.

You will find that I don't mention my sister Wendy much until later. Fact is she was always there, but just quiet. I don't remember a lot of interaction with her during those years.

My father was a truck driver and seemingly always on the road, so we saw very little of him. When he was home, he was sleeping. Robin and I had our moments like most siblings do, but I loved him very much and tried to be the big brother to him, rather than him to me.

Periodically throughout the summer, my mother dropped Robin and I off at the Barksdale Boy's Club. It was a place that young males could go and spend the day. It had many recreational things to do, such as table tennis, bumper pool, basketball and jumping on a huge trampoline.

One day while at the safe-haven and during lunch hour, box lunches were provided and passed out to everyone. While eating a sandwich, I noticed a couple of kids picking on Robin and trying to take his meal, so I walked over.

"Leave my brother alone."

Robin was actually prepared to let them have his lunch. I told you that he had more common sense then I did.

It was shortly thereafter that I found myself running away from the club and down the street, because the boys started to chase me with sticks in their hands. Though pudgy, I was running pretty fast, but breathing heavily while I staved off their pursuit of me.

A Father's Double Life

I ran a whole block and as the punks were gaining on me, I arrived at the corner of Barksdale and Peabody when I made the decision to go into a public library, figuring that they wouldn't follow me in there, because you had to be quiet.

I was sweating profusely while getting closer to the main entrance when I looked over my shoulder only to see them right on my tail. I opened the glass door and made it through the first set of double doors just fine, but with my force from running, in conjunction with my sweaty palms while trying to open the second door, my left hand slipped off the handle and right through the glass, shattering it instantly.

A large piece of glass then descended, (resembling the scene in the movie *"Ghost"* when Patrick Swayze's friend is killed while trying to get out of a window, when a swinging hook shatters the upper glass and sends a jagged edge down, killing him instantly) and therefore, slicing my wrist, nearly missing a main artery. An initial spurt of blood shot a foot into the air and then continued to flow. My body was soon covered in my own tide of crimson.

I stood there in shock while screaming,

"Help me! Help me!"

While holding my left wrist with my right hand, I watched the hot, red lava pour from my body, when this white man took off his shirt, wrapped it around my wrist and applied pressure to limit the bleeding. I guess the boys who were chasing me backed off once the glass broke. An ambulance then arrived and took me to the hospital where I was cleaned up, stitched up and allowed to go home with my mother who arrived shortly thereafter.

I could hear her voice, before she entered the room where I was being treated. She sounded hysterical.

Hysterical, now there's a unique word. It is the only word that I know of, that can have totally opposite meanings, either ecstatically happy or emotionally upset; just a thought.

My mother of course, was upset. She entered the room crying and carrying on while she hugged and kissed me,

"Are you okay sweetheart?"

"I'm okay mom."

"Are you sure?"

"I'm okay."

"You are a tough little boy," she said, while I sat there calm as could be.

I was starting to think that I had nine lives, for that was the second life threatening event that I had experienced. I only had seven more left.

Chapter 5
Embarrassing Moments

It was in August of 1977 when tragic news struck millions of fans around the world as Elvis Presley's death at the age of forty-two was officially announced on August 16th. He was found dead on his bathroom floor at Graceland by his then fiancée, Ginger Alden.

Elvis Presley was to the 60's and 70's, what Michael Jackson was to the 80's and 90's, and therefore a musical legend, with his gyrating hips and embroidered jump suits.

The news filled the airwaves and was by far, the biggest media story of my life at that point. Within days, the long funeral procession of white limos was shown on national television as it drove down Elvis Presley Boulevard, on its way to Forest Hill Cemetery, only a couple of miles from our house. Again, I was only eleven, but old enough to know what a tragic loss he was to the world; I stayed glued to the television along with my parents.

A short time after Elvis was laid to rest, some idiots tried to steal his body from the mausoleum and he was reburied at Graceland; the world had lost an iconic figure.

The summer of 1977 officially ended and it was time to start my sixth grade year at Dunn Elementary. Dunn was a one-story brick building and not very modern. It looked old and run down, kind of like the rest of Memphis at the time; Ms. Marian was my teacher. She was a tall, slender, brown-skinned lady and wore an Afro. That was the in-thing in the seventies.

Michael Cavicante

DUNN ELEMENTARY SCHOOL

My very first crush of a girl my own age was on Nannette. She was a black girl with a beautiful, mocha complexion. She had silky, ebony hair and wore it pulled back in a ponytail. She normally wore what resembled overalls with a nice blouse underneath. She had a mole on her forehead and was precious, but I was really shy as a kid and never approached girls.

I would see her walking home from school and tried to get her attention at times, but she never paid me any mind, actually rolling her eyes at me at times, but I still thought she was cute nonetheless. Just looking at her was enough for me. I usually lagged behind her about a hundred feet or so, just so she could stay in my sight, but she would eventually get home while I would still have another mile or so to walk before reaching my destination.

As indicated before, I was quite pudgy by eleven years old and therefore started to develop quite a complex about myself. My mother didn't make my complex any better when shopping for clothes she would always referred to me as husky. She would say it loud too, so everyone in the store heard her when she spoke.

"You know you can't get into those pants son, you wear husky size!"

Boy, are you talking about being embarrassed. I wanted to bury my head in the sand.

While we are on the subject of embarrassing moments, any chances for a friendship with Nannette were probably thwarted when one day while in class, I felt a weird sensation in my leg and it started to shake. I had never felt that feeling before and stood up while trying to walk it off.

"*What's wrong Michael?*" my teacher asked.

"*I don't know ma'm, but my leg feels funny. May I step into the hallway for a few minutes?*"

"*Sure you can.*" She then escorted me to the door with a deep look of concern on her face.

"*Are you okay Michael?*"

"*I don't know. My legs feel numb and are tingling.*"

She allowed me to walk the hallway until the numbness and tingling subsided. I then went back into the classroom and took a seat.

She continued with her teachings, but only minutes after taking my seat, my left leg got that funny sensation again, so I tried to stand up while other kids in the classroom looked on. All of a sudden and while standing, I clutched my desk while falling to the floor.

"*Help me. What's wrong with me?*" I exclaimed

I heard fellow classmates laughing as I went into a convulsion; it felt really weird, the convulsion that is.

The best way I can describe the feeling is like my legs were detached from my body and floating around me. I had absolutely no control over what was happening and it seemingly lasted forever.

I woke up hours later in the hospital and was given an EEG (Electroencephalogram) the following day to test my brain waves. Sure enough, I was diagnosed with Epilepsy and what I had experienced was a Grand-Mal Seizure which was the more severe of the two types of seizures that Epileptics have; the less severe being Petite Mal.

I was prescribed Phenobarbital to take three times a day and was able to go back to school immediately, but now felt uneasy around my classmates. I thought they would make fun of me because of what happened, but to my recollection, no one ever did.

As of matter of fact, as the school year continued, we had weekly or monthly awards and if you won, your picture was posted on the door with adjectives that described you pasted around your picture. Well, I won one month, if not two months, for most likable and most friendly, which I considered to be an honor.

I went on to have many seizures over the course of the next five years, because the medication didn't always work. The seizures mostly happened while I was asleep. I would awaken in the middle of the night knowing that I was about to have one, because they always started in my legs.

I always yelled out for my mother while getting out of bed and trying to stand up, but would then fall to the floor as the seizure continued. I slept for hours after having one and always woke up with a terrible headache, but every time I woke up, my mother was right by my side. The one that I had in school was the only one that I would ever have in public, thank God.

Though the drug limited my seizures, Phenobarbital had terrible side effects. I was falling down the stairs all of the time, because it threw off my equilibrium. I was also banging my head into the walls on purpose and acting crazy. I was eventually switched to Dilantin and all of those bizarre things stopped happening. Aside from the Epilepsy, I was very prone to injuries.

After school, Willie and I, along with other neighborhood kids regularly played football in a grassy field close to my house. My mother never liked the idea of me playing sandlot football and had warned me on more than one occasion, but I loved the sport and couldn't help myself.

Willie and I normally played for opposite teams to make it even, because we were both pretty good. Chris (Willie's brother) always picked me, because I had exceptional hands, so he knew if he threw it to me, I was going to catch it. I was also big and it always took two or more guys to tackle me if I was carrying the football.

Well one day, we were playing football when I caught a pass from Chris and continued running. Willie, who was very fast, caught me from behind, wrapped me up and tried to tackle me, but I must have dragged him five yards or so, before others piled on top of me. After carrying the pile another ten yards, I was finally tackled and my left shoulder was driven into the ground with all of that weight on top of me.

I knew something was wrong when I got up, because I couldn't move my left arm. The football game was officially over. Willie walked me home and into the arms of my mother.

"What's wrong with him?"
"I don't know ma'm, but he can't move his left arm."
"Michael, what's wrong?"
"I don't know mom, but it hurts a lot."

She tried to lift it up at which point I screamed in agony. I knew at that point that I was about to hear the *"I told you so speech."* Willie then left to head home.

"I told you about playing sandlot football."
"I know mother," I responded calmly.
"I just knew something like this was going to happen eventually."

I was silent while she prepared to take me to the hospital. After we got into the car, she preached some more while I just listened.

After arriving at the Emergency Room and being seen by a doctor, I was diagnosed with a broken growth line/plate and had to wear a contraption that kept my left arm suspended in the air, while bent at the elbow, hand facing forward. The bottom of the device was strapped around my ribcage and stomach to provide support.

I wore the device for six to eight weeks and had to sleep in a chair. Bathing was difficult because I had to temporarily remove the brace and bathe with one arm, not being able to move my left arm at all. The injury would inhibit the growth of my left arm and cause it to be almost two inches shorter than my right arm moving into adulthood.

I wasn't joked about the epileptic seizure that I had in school, but I was definitely joked about the contraption that I had to wear for my injury. All I needed was one for my right arm and I would have resembled a mummy. It was all in good fun though. I didn't let the jokes bother me.

While in the sixth grade, I was doing exceptional on spelling tests while scoring perfectly on just about all of them. If I didn't score one hundred percent, I still scored in the mid to high nineties. Those high scores would have me nominated for the Dunn Elementary Spelling Bee. I don't know where my knack for being able to spell came from; I guess it was a natural ability. With that being said, I was honored to participate and wanted to do well.

The spelling bee was held in the cafeteria, but I didn't last long in the competition. After getting only two or three words correct, I was stumped with the next word.

"Michael, spell kernel."

I thought to myself, *"That is easy."*

"K-E-R-N-E-L" I responded.

"No Michael, that is kernel as in a kernel of corn. I will use it in a sentence for you."

After she used the word in a sentence, I was still befuddled. I had only seen the word spelled one way, but tried again.

"K-E-R-N-A-L?"

"That is incorrect. The word is spelled, C-O-L-O-N-E-L. I'm sorry Michael. Thanks for participating."

"You're welcome." I responded.

But then I wondered, *"How in the world do you get an "R" sound out of that spelling?*

Michael Cavicante

While heading back to my classroom, I was sad, because it was an event that I thought I was going win with ease, but instead was one of the first contestants eliminated. The only good thing that came from it was that I have never had a problem spelling the word Colonel ever again. It was etched in my memory forever.

I finished my sixth grade year in May of 1978 without ever making Nannette's acquaintance. I was twelve years old and just looking forward to the summer. Willie and I had grown closer. I guess he was like the older brother that I really didn't have.

Our new thing was walking down the street and trying to sing the Temptations hit, *"My Girl"*. I don't know why we picked that song in particular, but we sang it quite often while trying to harmonize a cappella. We both thought that we could sing and had the impression that we sounded great; again, that was our impression.

Other than being close with Willie, I wanted a ten-speed bike. All of the kids in the neighborhood had one and I knew that we were of limited means, but that doesn't stop a kid from wanting. I was mature for my age and really hadn't asked for anything since asking for my own song several years prior. I knew that my family couldn't afford it, but my mother knew that I wanted a new bike.

Miraculously one day, she brought one home; I never will forget it. It was bright orange and fully equipped with a horn, reflectors, streamers and even a headlight. It was the nicest thing I had ever been given. I had owned only one bike in my short life and it had foot brakes. It therefore took me a while to adjust to having handbrakes like a ten-speed does. Yeah, I'm leading to something here.

I was riding my new bike all over the neighborhood every day, all day, when one day, I was riding on Ball Road. The street started level coming into the neighborhood, but then came a steep downward hill and afterwards, leveled off again.

I was getting up speed in preparation to descend the hill. I was flying when I hit the top of the hill and started my rapid descent. With the wind in my face, smiling from ear to ear and riding with no hands, I was leaning back casually on my perch. I was easily going about thirty-five miles per hour and felt like a king, when suddenly a car pulled out of a driveway.

"Holy shit!" I said out loudly, which was uncommon coming from my mouth, because I didn't swear.

My handlebars started to wobble and I dropped down to grab them immediately in order to control the steering. I panicked and tried to stop the bike with my foot brakes, which I didn't have and couldn't figure out why the stupid thing wasn't stopping. By the time I figured it out, it was too late. No, I didn't hit the car, but instead, guided the bike sharply left into a yard to avoid hitting the vehicle. It was a narrow miss by inches.

The turn was so sharp that I practically did a U-turn onto those premises while totally out of control. A practically inanimate object eventually stopped me. It was a barbed-wire fence.

To say the least, I ruined my bike, flattened both tires and shredded my left forearm to pieces. I had become so accustomed to physical pain, I didn't even cry. When I looked down and saw my arm torn to pieces, I just thought to myself,

"Just another battle scar in the life of Michael Cavicante."

Not a tear was shed or scream let out; I had become immune to pain. I was actually more upset about my bike being damaged than I was about my injury, but while bleeding profusely, I walked my wreck of a bike home, only a block away.

After arriving home minutes later, my mother took care of me after I told her what had happened. She became hysterical. There's that word again.

"Dammit, why do you keep hurting yourself?"
"Calm down mom, I am okay."
"Well I'm not okay. Do you have a death wish or something?"
"No."
"What are you trying to do my son? Why are you always hurting yourself?"
"A car pulled out in front of me, so I had to turn into a yard."
"What could have possibly done this to your arm? You look like you've been in a knife fight."
"It was a barbed-wire fence."

I sat there while my mother cleaned the wounds and applied Betadine. That was my mom's answer for any type of bruise, cut, etc. Betadine and a band-aid, but in this case with the scars being so long and broad, I needed gauze. Yeah, the ugly marks are still there. I probably should have had stitches and the imperfections wouldn't look as bad as they do now.

It was also that summer when I met Landry. He was a tall, thin, dark-skinned, black guy who wore a big Afro and always had a pick stuck in the back of it. Everything seemed fine one day while shooting hoops over Andrew's house. He was laughing and joking throughout, but when we were done, he started hitting me for no apparent reason. I didn't fight back and just fell to the ground into the fetal position in order to protect myself as he started stomping my head into the ground, literally.

Michael Cavicante

WILLIE, MY CHILDHOOD FRIEND

Willie, my guardian angel, was there to stop Landry from mistreating me and stood between his foot and my head.

"Landry, stop man. He ain't done nothing to you."
"That nigga is a punk; look at 'em."
"He just doesn't like to fight, now leave him alone man."

Landry finally stopped and I stood up with grass and leaves in my hair while crying like a big ole baby. I also happened to look up and saw Chandra standing in the doorway. She was Andrew's sister and very pretty. Needless to say, I felt embarrassed to have been beaten up in front of her.

While wallowing in my self-pity, he continued to call me "*punk*" and other names; I just stood there and took it. After a few minutes, I turned and walked home by myself. I was hoping it was a onetime thing, but it happened almost every time he saw me.

The word soon got out around the neighborhood that I wouldn't fight, so eventually, I became the neighborhood punching bag and that would go on for a while as I was beat up by Donald who was half my size and his friend Dick periodically; oh yeah let's not forget Landry. It was sad now that I look back at it, because I was a good kid and never did anything to hurt anybody.

A Father's Double Life

The summer of 1978 ended and I started the seventh grade. I was enrolled and bussed to Oakhaven Junior High in September of that year. It was a huge school in the middle of another nice neighborhood, not too far away from Memphis International Airport. It was several stories high, all brick and looked grand. It had a separate detached gymnasium and auditorium located in the rear of the school as well as an ROTC building. It also had separate buildings for music class and wood shop. Oakhaven Junior High and High School were combined, so even though I was in the seventh grade, I was attending school with high school kids.

It was the first predominately white school that I had gone to and therefore was my first real introduction to white kids; they were so darned cool. We acted the same, talked the same, and even liked the same types of music, but as I grew up, I learned to appreciate just about every genre of music, and yes, even country.

My brother had already been attending Oakhaven for a year, but again, was in Special Education classes. The compassion that kids had when we were younger was non-existent during our high school years. In conjunction with being mentally challenged, he wore glasses with super-thick lenses, and because he had a bad temper, my brother would often break his glass frame and would have to duct tape them down the middle, so that didn't help his cause. He was teased unmercifully.

I tried to take up for him, but again, didn't like to fight, so it was always verbally. It wasn't easy going to junior high and having to deal with my brother being picked on.

On the flip side of the coin and for some reason, white kids just loved, if not adored me. I also enjoyed riding the school bus and was making new friends. Yep, it seems like everything all of a sudden was looking up for me. That was until my father got a wild hair up his butt.

At that point in my life, I wished that my parents could afford for us to wear designer clothes, but name brands such as Nike, Member's Only, Levi's, IZOD, Stacy Adams, Polo, and others, would only be a dream. I saw other kids wear nice clothes and could do nothing but admire the pretty young girls that wore the tight jeans of Gloria Vanderbilt and Jordache. I always made sure that I walked slowly behind them in the hallways while admiring the view. Yes, I was at the age when I was starting to wonder about the other sex.

While my curiosity in females was on the rise, I also had wishes that we lived in a nice air-conditioned house and that I had my own bedroom with a door that I could close for privacy. Yes, there were a lot of things that I longed for and therefore desired, but for the most part I was content. I guess mainly because I had no other choice.

I thought about what it might have been like to have a girlfriend. It's hard not to when you are in high school. I was walking down the halls between classes while seeing boys and girls hugged up against the lockers and kissing. How could I not wonder? But thought to myself, but what girl in their right mind would want me? I wore no-name jeans, no-name shirts, no-name shoes and socks with holes throughout. For cologne, I used my father's cheap after-shave. On top of all that, I was a coward and didn't like to fight. What girl would have anything to do with the likes of me?

I was at the age where I was starting to get curious about myself. Hair started to grow in places that I didn't know hair was supposed to be. I liked girls, but still didn't have a clue about sex, nor was I really interested at the time. I just wanted a girl as a friend, that's all; just a pretty face of the opposite sex to talk to.

I was at the age where I wanted the family to sit down at the table and have dinner together. I wanted my dad to spend time with me, but if he wasn't on the road driving his truck, his time at home was spent in bed sleeping. When he was home and awake, he was watching television and therefore planted on the couch in the living room where the television existed. He routinely watched such shows as 60 minutes, Hee-Haw and Lawrence Welk on the weekends and rarely if ever, spent any quality time with any of us.

To make matters worse, there was only one television in the house and he had total control of it when he was home. Robin and I would often turn the channel if we saw him sleeping at which point he would wake up.

"Turn my program back on, I wasn't sleep."

My father did like punching me and Robin in the arm or chest with his fist when we walked pass him, and at times—he knocked the wind right out of us. That was his weird way of showing affection I guess, because he never hugged, or told us that he loved us.

He never sat at the table and ate. Mom always served him in the living room when he was at home. I remember times when eating, a Tampon Commercial would air and he would say,

"God Darnit. Why did they have to show that while I was eating?" as if the network knew exactly when my father would be enjoying his meal.

Yep, my father was quite the character and it would be his character that would come into question in the future years as my world would be rocked by the upcoming events and I would never be the same again.

Chapter 6
A Father's Betrayal

As we moved into 1979, my dad approached me one day, when he started talking to me about girls and wanted to know if I was interested in them.

"*So, do you have a girlfriend yet?*"
"*No dad, I don't have a girlfriend.*"
"*Do you like girls?*"
"*Yeah, I like 'em.*"
"*Then why don't you have a girlfriend?*"
"*I don't know.*"
"*Have you had sex yet?*"
"*No dad, I have never had sex.*"
"*Don't you ever wonder about it?*"
"*Not really. I guess I don't really understand it.*"
"*Hmmm.*" he muttered.

The conversations made me feel uncomfortable. Even though I did like girls, I hadn't really thought about sex. These conversations continued periodically over the months to come.

It was still early 1979 when my mother ended up in the hospital for her diabetes. She had been a diabetic since 1969. I just hadn't brought it up until this point, because it had been a non-issue, but she was taking insulin shots daily.

She passed out one day and was taken to the hospital via ambulance. All the family was devastated as our beloved mother was no longer at home.

I was really forced to mature even more so, because my father was always on the road. I had a little sister and mentally challenged brother to care for while my dad was busy earning a living. I had learned how to cook a little, just from helping my mother out in the kitchen. I had helped her cook dinner some nights and breakfast on the weekends. I also helped her bake cakes during the holidays, probably because I liked eating the batter, before and after we poured it into the pan, so I had an idea of how to put a meal together.

Every morning, I awoke Robin and Wendy in order to get them ready for school and made sure they washed up and brushed their teeth. Robin was going on fourteen and already tall and thin. Again, he wore thick glasses as he had always had poor vision and sucked his thumb well into his early twenties.

Robin was also a bed-wetter and it drove my parents crazy. Even though it was my mother that had to launder his sheets and air the mattress, it was my father that at times beat him for wetting the bed, but the lashings helped very little as Robin continued over the years to come. His room would reek of urine as I had to walk through his sleeping quarters in order to get downstairs, at times holding my breath so I didn't have to inhale the stench.

Wendy was nine years old, growing fast and blossoming into a beautiful girl. She was light-skinned, thin and very pretty.

Even though I had developed many household skills, I had no idea on how to do a girl's hair. I attempted to comb and style Wendy's hair in the mornings while she yelled in pain.

"Be still Wendy."

"Ouch! That hurts Michael."

"Be still Wendy, it won't take long."

"Stop Michael, you're hurting my head."

I eventually finished and braided her hair into three pigtails, one on each side of her head, and one in the back. I thought it looked pretty good if I had to say so myself, even though nobody else thought so.

When my father came off road trips, I had dinner cooked and he was quite impressed. I had such dishes such as pork chops, macaroni and cheese and green beans prepared. Doesn't sound like a poor man's meal, huh? Please don't get it twisted. You see my father had mom buy food that was designated just for him. It didn't mean that the rest of the family would enjoy the same delicacies. He also loved strawberries and whipped cream, but kept them in his own little refrigerator in their bedroom, along with his personal stash of milk and beer. That fridge was off limits to everyone else.

A Father's Double Life

I served his dinner while he sat on the couch watching the tube, just as my mother had done every night he was home. When he finished, I took his plate and glass and then washed the dishes, but after Robin and Wendy also finished their meals; we sat at the dining room table. My father was pretty much a *"Do as I say, not as I do"* type guy, but we respected him immensely.

I guess for my father, maybe I was becoming a little too much like the woman of the house. One night, I lay asleep in my bed, when my father came up to my room and awakened me. It was about one in the morning and of course, Robin and Wendy were sleeping as well.

"Michael, wake up." he whispered loudly into my ear while shaking me lightly.

"What's going on?" I asked, as I sat up on an elbow, while rubbing my eyes with my other hand.

"Get out of bed and come downstairs."

"Why?"

"I've got something that I want to show you, so get up."

After making sure I was awake and getting up, my father headed back downstairs.

Still half asleep, I pushed my covers back and slowly got out of bed. I then grabbed my robe and blindly found my way downstairs. After arriving into the living room, he approached me,

"Go take a shower and wash up good."

"Why do I have to take a shower in the middle of the night?"

"Don't ask a bunch of questions; just do what I ask you to."

"Well, I need to go back upstairs and get a change of underwear."

"No you don't, just take a shower, okay?"

"Okay dad."

After being fully awakened by the water of the shower hitting my face, I bathed myself thoroughly as my father had asked of me, but was wondering why I needed to take a shower for him to show me something. After turning off the faucet and exiting the tub, he came to the door and cracked it open.

"Make sure to put some powder between your legs."

"Okay dad."

It was at this point that I knew something wasn't right with the chain of events that was taking place. I became frightened while I patted my face dry with the towel and then dried the rest of my body. As my father requested, I rubbed baby powder between my legs, but was stalling. I knew something was wrong and wasn't anxious to leave the bathroom.

"What is going on?" I thought to myself.
"What is my father about to do to me?"

Those questions would be answered soon enough as he came yet again to the bathroom door.

"What's taking you so long? Come on out of there."
"Okay dad, I'm coming."

I put my robe on and opened the door while turning off the light. He grabbed my hand and led me to his bedroom. The lights were off, but the room was dimly lit by the use of a night-light plugged into the wall. As we walked in, he closed the door behind us.

"Go ahead and lie on the bed, but on your back."
"Okay."

After doing so, I watched him walk slowly towards me. He had nothing on but his customary boxers and his stomach was protruding. He had started to develop quite a gut and looked quite disgusting.

I lie on the bed, holding my robe closed and as he moved my hands, I felt the bed give in, while he lied next to me. He then pulled my robe open and the next thing I knew, I felt his hands around my penis and then his mouth while I lie there motionless.

The room was pretty dark, but the night-light allowed me to see enough. I lifted my head to observe what was happening when I saw his head going up and down while performing fellatio on me. I laid my head back down and allowed him to continue while staring at the ceiling.

Was I so frightened of my father that I couldn't tell him to stop, or was I just naïve and thought that what he was doing was natural? Whatever the reason, I allowed him to continue. I felt helpless and didn't know what to do. All kinds of thoughts were going through my head and it felt like I was in the middle of a nightmare. After several minutes, I felt a sensation that I had never felt before. I didn't know what it was at the time, because I had never so much as masturbated, but I was about to experience my first ever orgasm.

I must admit, it felt good, but I kept my emotions to myself. I wanted to moan, but didn't. My body became tense and stiff at the very moment I was about to climax and I guess my father sensed it, because he took his mouth off of my penis and finished jacking me off. Upon the release, I felt the urge to scream, but didn't while just holding my emotions inside. I then felt wetness hit my legs and stomach, but didn't know what it was.

My father finished, got up and turned on the lights, while I lifted my head and looked down, wondering what the white stuff all over me was.

"What has just happened?" I asked.

"You just had an orgasm," he replied as he went on to explain it to me.

"Okay."

"Did you like it?"

"I don't know."

"What do you mean you don't know?"

"Are we supposed to be doing this dad?"

"There isn't anything wrong with what just happened, just don't tell your mother."

"Okay, I won't tell her."

"Are you okay?"

"Yes, I'm okay."

Of course I told him that, but I was anything but okay and really disturbed by what had just transpired. He went to the bathroom while I lie there on the bed. He soon came back with a damp, hot rag and wiped me off thoroughly.

"So tell me, did you enjoy it?"

"I don't know dad."

He then became very angry.

"Awe... take your ass to bed."

Without saying another word, I got up and departed the room. I went back upstairs and got in the bed, but lay there thinking about what had just happened. Eventually, I went to sleep.

From that night on, I felt awkward around him. I still respected him, but didn't know how to perceive him.

The next several weeks went by and he left on his road trips and returned, but our relationship was definitely different. It was really weird, almost like I had taken the place of my mother. I would be cooking in the kitchen and he would come in there and slap me on the butt and look over my shoulder while I tended to the food. It was almost like he wanted to kiss me while he talked softly,

"So, when is dinner going to be ready?"

"Soon." I replied

"Boy, you are one healthy young man," while he had a hand on my waist as he took a step back to observe the rear of me.

It was really crazy, like a homosexual relationship was developing. I felt so uncomfortable, but was clueless on what to do, or how to handle the situation.

Well, another week or so went by and I was again sleeping in my bed when I am awakened by my father's mouth on my penis. I woke up terrified while trying to push him away.

"*What are you doing?*" I said, while trying not to raise my voice to awaken my brother.

"*Be still.*"

"*Stop dad.*"

"*Shut up.*" He said.

It was dark in the room, but I heard Robin turning in his bed. I started crying silently while my father was again between my legs. I felt his elbows force my legs open wider so he could lie there. He continued while I squirmed in the bed, but he wasn't going to stop and sucked my penis like a mad man. Robin soon called my name,

"*Michael?*"

"*Yes Robin.*" I answered in a whimper as my father stopped momentarily.

"*Are you okay?*"

"*Yes Robin, I'm fine. Go back to sleep.*"

"*Okay*" he replied.

My father continued, while I lay there with my emotions breaking down. It seemed as if it lasted forever, maybe because that time was much worse than the first, because that time it was just taken like I was being raped.

I cried silently while he performed oral sex on me, until I eventually and finally climaxed, but again, showed no emotion as he then got up and walked away. He didn't ask if I was okay, didn't say goodnight, or that he was sorry, nothing; he just walked away.

I then realized that there was no semen on me, at which point I also realized that I must have ejaculated into my father's mouth. Had he swallowed my sperm? What in the world was going on and what would become of this crazy and bizarre situation?

I just lay there and cried myself back to sleep, after pulling my underwear back up, the covers back over me and without bothering to wipe myself off. I held those covers so tightly to my body as if they were going to protect me from that ever happening again.

I woke up the next day, grabbed some underclothes, went downstairs and took a bath. While passing my father en route to the bathroom, he had the nerve to speak.

"*Good morning.*"

"*Good morning,*" I replied; but there wasn't anything good about it.

I couldn't believe that he had the audacity to even speak to me. There was seemingly no shame on his part and he even had the nerve to have a grin on his face while sitting on the couch reading the newspaper.

"What was wrong with this man?" I thought to myself.

After getting to the lavatory, I shut the door behind me. I wanted to lock it, but there was no latch on the door. I just wanted to shut myself off from the rest of the world, but I couldn't. I wanted to seclude myself in that 4 x 6 hole of a room and never come out. I ran my bathwater and while it ran, I looked in the mirror and wondered why my life was in the disarray that it was and was there anyway I could get the hell out of it.

Standing there naked, I looked at my body and hated it. My left forearm looked horrible from the crash with the barbed wire fence; the inside of my left wrist had been gashed by glass and was unsightly; my stomach still showed the burn markings from falling over that gas heater; my knees were all scarred up from the falls on those skates; and my shoulder still had pain in it.

The only thing that wasn't scarred was my innocent face as I looked into the mirror, but I guess in a way, it too was scarred. For when in the presence of my classmates and friends, I wore a smile, or at least tried to anyway, but inside and behind the facade, there was a world of hurt and pain that nobody but me could ever know.

The song, *"Tracks of my Tears"* sung by Linda Ronstadt, which peaked at number twenty-five on the charts in 1975, would best describe what was going on with me. Every time I heard it, I thought of how life imitates art. It was certainly true in that case. The song was co-written by Smokey Robinson, Warren Moore and Mary Tarplin and sung by several artists, but I liked Ronstadt's version the best.

While still fixated on the reflection looking back at me, I asked myself;

Why was I born and why had God put me on this earth? Why did God allow me to be born to such a father? Why did he allow me to go through so much pain?

I felt as if I were dammed before my life ever began.

After I got through feeling sorry for myself, I got into the tub and just soaked; my body felt nasty and violated. While washing my penis, I looked at it and wondered why my father enjoyed putting his mouth on it. What joy was he getting out of doing what he did to me? Why would a father do this to his son?

As I scrubbed it, scrubbed it and scrubbed it some more, I broke down in tears, brought my legs up to my chest, rested my head on my knees and just cried. After several minutes, I finished washing, pulled the stopper and exited the tub. I grabbed my towel, dried myself off, put on my underclothes and again looked in the mirror.

There were no thoughts, no wishes, no dreams, or aspirations, just a blank stare. I felt empty and very sad, but thought to myself,

"Today is another day."

I brushed my teeth, put my robe on and walked out of the bathroom while trying to lift my own spirits.

My spirits would be lifted shortly thereafter, a couple of days later, when my mother was released from the hospital; she had been gone about six weeks. I was so happy to see her that I didn't know what to do, but didn't tell her about my father's transgressions. Would my father ever touch me again? I didn't know, but the damage to me was already done.

Chapter 7

Downward Spiral

In the following months, I started doing extremely badly in school. I wasn't necessarily an honor student, but I was far from failing either. I had showed a lot of promise and was raved on by my teachers throughout elementary school while earning decent marks up until that point, but all of a sudden, I started acting up, became talkative, got into it with other students, etc. I was looking for an outlet I guess, or better yet, attention.

I even let neighborhood bad boys, Donald and Dick, influence me into doing something really stupid while at Surplus City one day. It was a local discount store, nearby on Elvis Presley Boulevard. I actually don't know how I ended up there with them, but I did. They dared me to steal something and I don't even remember what it was. I think it was a candy bar or something very petty.

I took it, put it in my pocket and attempted to walk out of the store, but was caught at the door by security. The police were called and I was handcuffed and taken to Juvenile Hall.

I never will forget those handcuffs being clanked on my wrist and arms twisted behind my back, only to clank the other hand; they hurt and were really tight. They also bend your wrist back in an awkward position to put them on. I was put into the back seat of the police car, but leaned forward and to the side in order to keep my hands from being pinned between my body and the back of the seat.

Once at Juvenile Hall, my mother was called while I sat in an office and waited. She came and got me out as I was released without incident, but of course, she lectured me all the way home. I guess the store decided not to press charges.

My mental troubles continued while one day on the late bus after school. I was in spring training trying out for Junior Varsity Football. I said something disrespectful to the bus driver, Ms. Young, and she took me back to the school and dropped me off, so I had no way of getting home.

With my life in disarray and confusion, I sat on the curb in front of the school and became angry while wondering why all of those things were happening to me.

I had no one to talk to, not even Willie. Maybe I could have talked to him, but I was too embarrassed to share the disgusting information. Even if I did have someone neutral to talk to, would I? No, that wasn't me. I was the type of person that was just going to keep it to myself. No one needed to know what was going on with me and even if I wanted to tell someone, whom could I turn to? Who could actually help me? Who would understand or better yet, who would even believe me?

I felt lost, confused, angry, isolated, depressed and yes, even suicidal, but I loved life and people too much to ever come to such a pass, so a mere thought is all it would ever be.

Wanting and needing to vent some frustration, I picked up some rocks and started to throw them at the school windows, eventually breaking one. Almost immediately after hearing the shattering of the glass, a guy came out of a nearby house and saw me. As he and another guy started chasing me, I ran.

We were in Memphis, the deep south—and the only thing that was going through my head at that point, about a couple of white men chasing me, was that they were going to hang me or give me thirty lashes with a whip. I had all of a sudden become Kunta Kinte in the movie, *"Roots"*. The hit mini-series of the seventies had left a lasting impression on me and just how mean and cruel one race can be towards another.

They yelled *"Stop!"* and only my fear of being gunned down by undercover KKK members caused me to halt in my tracks. Just as Kunta had surrendered, I fell to my knees and held my hands interlocked on the back of my head while they approached me from behind.

As my eyes filled with tears, I looked up at the sky, but then closed my eyes while I heard them talking. They would detain me until police arrived and guess what? Yep! I was taken back to Juvenile Hall and held until my mother came and picked me up.

I am sure my mother was wondering what the heck had happened to her precious son, for it seemed I had taken a turn for the worse. My father never said a thing; maybe because in the back of his mind, he knew what had happened to me. After all, he was the cause of it all.

I was suspended from school for several days for vandalism and my mother had to go to the Board of Education to get the expulsion cleared.

The school board recommended that I get psychiatric treatment. My dad was still working for Gordon's at the time which was part of the Teamsters Union, so he had great benefits. It was with those benefits that I was admitted into Mid-South's Hospital fifth floor Psychiatric Ward after my Seventh Grade year in 1979. The hospital was located not far from St. Jude Cancer Research Hospital near Downtown Memphis. I could actually see it from my bedroom window.

My psychologist was Dr. Stein, a big, tall, white man who wore Buddy Holly glasses. The ward itself was a regular hospital floor, with one long corridor and a nurse's station in the middle. The boys' rooms were at one end of the hallway and the girls' on the other, separated by the nurse's station. The emergency exits were locked. There was no way out.

During the day, we sat in the lounge which was pretty big. The ward consisted of about forty patients. We were escorted downstairs by the orderlies to the dining area to eat our meals which were three squares a day. That was the only time that we weren't held within the confines of the fifth floor. No playtime outside, no field trips or other excursions. It seemed almost as if we were in jail, but instead a minimum-security complex.

During the day, there were group counseling sessions as well as individual ones with our psychologist throughout the week.

I met with Dr. Stein periodically and we sat down and talked. He asked me about my thoughts, my dreams, ambitions, etc. I even took that Rorschach inkblot test which is an exam given by Psychologists to help determine the personality characteristics and emotional functions of their patients which I never found out or knew the results of.

He also of course asked me about my home life, but in all the counseling sessions I attended both in-group and with Dr. Stein, I never shared with them what my father had done to me; it never came out. I guess because I was too afraid what would happen if I told anybody, so I just kept it to myself and dealt with it the best that I could.

Some of the most memorable patients of the Psych Ward were; a black guy named Tyrell who could walk the whole length of the corridor on his hands. There was another guy called Tappy; I hope that was his nickname. He went into violent rages and often had to be secluded and given a shot.

Being secluded meant being held down by the orderlies and having your ankles and wrists cuffed to your bed as well as being often sedated with a shot.

Every bed in the ward had green ankle and wrist cuffs attached. They had locks on them and were made off some type of green, durable, thick, plastic, composite material. Sometimes when they cuffed you, you were secluded all night. It was something I hoped would never happen to me.

There was a girl named Katherine who was a pretty, redheaded, white girl. I remember her vividly for some reason. Maybe because like me, she too had Epilepsy, as I recall her having a seizure during in-group counseling one day.

There was this guy named Dre. He was an intimidating figure as he was a big, muscular, dark-skinned, black guy that wore a hair net. He also had a gold tooth in his mouth which was the first time I had ever seen that.

Then there was Beverly. She was a model thin, blonde hair, blue-eyed, white girl, who was very sweet. It was Beverly who I talked to and hung out with most of the time during the day. As you will discover, I didn't discriminate when it came to girls. I liked them and they liked me, but was shy and obviously mentally disturbed, so the girl always had to initiate any verbal contact with me.

There isn't a lot to tell about my stay at Mid-South thanks to the everyday ritual and routine. If I had to pick a highlight, it would that of being introduced to Pink Floyd's *"Another Brick in the Wall"*. I think it was the anthem of the Psych Ward because it was a new song that came out during my stay and played a lot by a guy who had a boom box. The song was rocking and even though none us were on drugs, well, not anything such as marijuana, opium, hash, PCP, LSD, Quaaludes, Preludes, heroine, etc.; but we could have been on medication prescribed by our doctors, which could have included any of the aforementioned.

Whenever the song blared out in the lounge, all of us kids were moving our head to the beat, snapping our fingers and singing in unison, especially when the part of the song came, *"Leave us kids alone."* As we all shouted out and pointed at each other as the song rocked away, it definitely provided a temporary bonding moment for us all. I think the message was clear. All of us to a degree—just wanted to be left alone. It was the perfect song.

After spending my entire eighth grade year in an Insane Asylum, I was released in the summer of 1980 at the age of fourteen. I said my good-byes to everyone, especially Beverly. I would never see her or any of the other patients of Mid-South's Fifth Floor Psych Ward again.

Though I had gone through therapy, it was almost like I hadn't had any, because I never mentioned to anyone about what my father had done. I was still keeping it bottled up inside of me. However, Mid-South Hospital did teach me one thing and that was that I wasn't the only kid with problems. Other than that, a whole year of my childhood had been stripped away, if a childhood is what you wanted to call it.

Chapter 8
The Dallas Effect

After getting back home and being re-united with my family, Willie welcomed me back and told me about a summer job program, C.E.T.A. It stood for (Comprehensive Employment & Training Act) enacted in 1973. It was a program in Memphis to employ low-income kids for the summer.

I went downtown, filled out an application and just like that, I got hired. At fourteen years old, I had my first job, which would be working at a home for the elderly in North Memphis. I worked from eight in the morning until four in the afternoon. My tasks were sweeping, mopping, buffing and mowing the lawn.

I remember the first time I tried to operate that buffer. I squeezed the handle and it sent me flying across the room; almost through the wall. It took awhile for me to get used to using it, but when I finally did, it was actually kind of fun. As a matter of fact, it was so much fun, that I would re-buff the halls after buffing them. I buffed those floors so much that you could see your reflection.

After work, my mother picked me up in Jaws, which was still, our 1974 Pontiac Bonneville, but was sporting a new look because she had wrecked it. My parents didn't have insurance, so a big hole in the front grille from the accident existed. Let me rephrase that. A big whole existed in the front of the car where the grille used to be.

So imagine that, along with the old type of round double headlights on each side which looked like eyes and then the serrated, jagged edges

Michael Cavicante

that were left over from the outer frame of the where the grille used to be, that resembled teeth and voila—You've got JAWS.

While working, some of my less desirable duties included, cleaning up feces of some of the patients after they defecated in their beds. I didn't know what death actually smelled like, but it had to resemble the smell that I endured while working at that place. It saddened me to see those elderly people at the mercy of the nurses. At times, I witnessed very poor treatment of the tenants.

Who could put their parents in such a place and forget about them? I was a very compassionate person. Even after what my father had done, I couldn't have even allowed him to go to such a place.

I routinely had conversations with some of the residents and they claimed not to have been visited in months, some, even years. Who on earth could do this to their own parents? It was bad enough that they were sent to such a dungeon of a place, but then not to visit them. What a shame I thought to myself.

After three weeks of wincing through the smell of fecal matter, I finally got my first check because they held back a week; I was so happy that I could help out. The minimum wage was $3.10 per hour and I was working forty hours a week, so my first check, after taxes, was around two hundred dollars for two weeks work. My mother picked me up and I went to cash the check and gave all the money to her.

"Here honey, you take forty dollars for yourself," she said.
"No thanks mom, I'm okay. You keep it and put it to good use."
"Where did I get such a precious son?"
"Mom—I came out of your vagina."

She looked astonished for all of a second with her mouth wide open. I looked back at her and she just laughed, but then reached over and gave me a kiss and hug.

After several weeks, I realized that my brother had a new friend; his name was Richard. He was a hefty, very smart, sixteen year old, blonde-haired, blue-eyed, all-American white kid. You could tell instantly that he was well bred and above anything ghetto or at least that is how he carried himself. He seemed to be a nice guy, but very manipulative in reference to how he treated my brother. I actually thought he was a redneck and therefore only using Robin as his field Negro. Those were my initial thoughts of him.

Richard and his parents had actually been living across the street from us in their home since 1974, but because of my stay at Mid-South Hospital

A Father's Double Life

and my friendship with Willie, I had never met him. They also kind of kept to themselves.

Richard in my opinion was a brat. He had his own car that his parents gave him and at the time, Robin was very much into vehicles, so he gravitated towards him.

He had Robin doing everything under the sun, from washing his car, to taking out the trash, to raking his yard, to mowing his lawn, and Robin did it, because he would tell him,

"Okay Robbie, if you want to ride in my car, you've got to do this."

And Robin would do whatever he said, just so he could ride in his car.

The prime time, hit drama *"Dallas"* was a big television hit at the time. Well, Robin would start to refer to Richard as J.R., and the brat relished in it, so much to the degree that he even went and bought a hat resembling the one that Larry Hagman wore in the soap opera.

I despised the impudent child for how he manipulated Robin and gave him a piece of my mind on more than one occasion, but eventually, I realized and accepted that Robin was happy, and did those things willingly. My brother had no friends at all, so Richard was it for him.

Ultimately, my sentiments towards Richard would change, when one day Robin was setting up a contraption on the street.

There was this girl in the neighborhood with whom he had a crush on; her name was Pauline. She just happened to be close by talking to a friend while standing on the road. She was very pretty and had hazel eyes, but like my brother, was a little mentally slow. However, also like my sibling, was very smart in so many other ways.

The common sense that I have been bragging on throughout this story would take a vacation on that particular day. We had grown up watching daredevil Evil Knievel on television, and at the age of eight, back in 1974, my brother and I were mesmerized at his failed attempt to jump across The Snake River Canyon, but he had performed countless other successful stunts, before and after that nationally televised performance.

Robin was more easily influenced than I was and I guess he had thoughts of grandeur while also wanting to impress his love interest by emulating an Evil Knievel stunt. It actually turned into quite the spectacle as kids gathered around to witness the feat.

My brother got a piece of wood and set up a ramp while placing one end of the board upon several bricks; the other end resting on the pavement. He then rode his bike about a hundred feet, turned around and got up a head of steam. He was really moving when he approached the inclined plane. As Robin approached the ramp, ascended the ramp and then off the ramp, he went flying through the air as we awaited his landing, it wasn't pretty. Robin came down awkwardly, flipped head first over the handlebars and busted his forehead wide open.

Robin lay on the street bleeding and it was none other than Richard who was the first to help me get him into the house. Robin was seemingly in a state of shock. Richard helped my brother into Wendy's bedroom and onto her bed. He then covered Robin up with covers and commanded the scene while asking for towels, ice, and other items. It was then when I finally realized he wasn't a bad guy after all and really did care about Robin.

As Robin lie there, bleeding and in pain, the only thing he could think of, was to ask the question,

"Did she see me?" referring to the girl he was trying to show-off for.

"Yeah Robin, she saw you, and I'm sure you impressed her," I replied, while I held his hand.

"Oh, okay, that's good," he said, as Richard and I looked at each other and smiled.

Robin was eventually taken to the hospital and needed stitches. He would eventually be okay and thanks largely in part to Richard's course of actions. It was after that incident, that I finally accepted Richard as a friend and thanked him.

MY EVENTUAL CHILDHOOD FRIEND RICHARD A.K.A. J.R.

A Father's Double Life

Shortly thereafter, he invited and then took me to my first ever concert to see Barry Manilow at the Mid-South Coliseum which I enjoyed thoroughly. Richard also taught me how to play chess, but eventually stopped playing me, because I started to beat him regularly. Richard also eventually got a basketball goal put up in his backyard and we started playing at his house. Yeah, ole Richard turned out to be a pretty cool guy. We had gotten so close that I would go over his house in the mornings and we would walk to the bus stop together.

One morning, I went over to have breakfast with him, but he wasn't dressed yet, with only a robe on. I was sitting in the kitchen about to eat some cereal when Richard's mother, who just so happened to be, the sweetest, kindest, and most beautiful woman that you would ever want to meet, next to my mother of course, handed him a wet pair of jeans to wear.

I didn't understand, with only thirty minutes before having to be on the bus, how Richard was going to be able to wear those soaked and wet pants to school, but kept my mouth shut.

I then observed while he put them in a machine that I had never seen before. Within seemingly minutes, he took them out of the machine and the pants were totally dry. I was totally astonished. I didn't know such a machine even existed. He went to another room, put them on and was ready for school in no time.

I was so amazed that it was the only thing that I thought about all day long. I thought about it so much that when I came home from school, I told my mother.

"Mom, Mom, we have got to get one of those things that Richard has."

"What on earth are you talking about?"

"Richard put a pair of wet jeans in some machine this morning and in no time at all, they were dry."

"Oh, you're talking about a clothes dryer."

"I guess; can we get one?"

"We can't afford a dryer honey. We can barely pay the rent."

"But if we had one, you wouldn't have to hang clothes outside anymore, right?"

"No, I wouldn't, but we can't afford it. I wish we could, but we can't, okay?"

"Okay." As all of my excitement was zapped out of me, I hung my head and walked away.

My initial reaction to Richard was how I perceived him back then, but now that I think about it, I was probably jealous that he had taken my brother away from me while I was at Mid-South Hospital. So the truth was that I had resented him; that was until we made amends.

Outside of working my summer job and being concerned about Robin's well being, my only escape was when Willie and I went out to play.

One day, we were over Stacy's house playing basketball. Stacy was known as the neighborhood brat. He lived in a really nice house with central air conditioning, wore the alligator shirts, designer jeans, Nike shoes, etc. You know, all the nice stuff mentioned earlier that I wished I had. However, I was never the jealous type and always complimented him on the things that he had going for him.

He was a light-skinned, small in stature, cute, kind of a pretty boy and was always cracking jokes on me for the clothes that I wore as well as the holes in my shoes.

We finished playing basketball on that particular day when Stacy decided to pick up a skateboard and chase me around his backyard; as usual, I ran. In retrospect, I don't think he ever had any intentions of hitting me with it, he just thought it was funny to see me run from him. I ran around in circles when all of a sudden, Willie stopped me in my tracks.

"Mike, you have to stop running. The more you keep running, the more they're going to pick on you! You have to stop running and fight! Now turn around and fight!"

It was on that day when I believe I became a real fighter, both in life and with my fist as I turned towards Stacy.

"Let's fight." I said.

He approached me and I grabbed that skateboard from him, only after he swung it and missed. Okay, maybe he did intend to hit me with it. I then got a hold of his little butt and threw him to the ground. I must have let every ounce of frustration inside of me out on Stacy that day, while I pounded my fists with his face. Yeah, I said it the way I wanted to…LOL.

He offered seemingly little to no resistance, or it could have been that I just overpowered him with my size and strength. I had to be pulled off of him by the onlookers and was proclaimed the winner. Willie and I then left and headed to my house.

All of the kids who were there cheered and applauded. I don't know if they were happy to have seen me finally fight back, or if it was because maybe just a little, they also resented the spoiled brat of a kid and wanted to see him get beat up? Either way, it felt good to have finally stood up for myself.

After getting home, I said good-bye to Willie and entered the house. My father just happened to be at home and sitting in his customary spot on the sofa reading the newspaper.

"Hello dad."

He looked away from the newspaper and at me. Surprisingly, he folded the newspaper and sat it in his lap as if he was going to pay me some attention.

"Hey, what are you up to?"

"I just got in a fight and I won."

"Oh yeah, who did you beat up?"

"Stacy."

"You mean that little runt of a kid who's always making fun of you?"

"Yeah, that's the one."

"Well hell, you should have beaten him up; you're twice his size."

He then picked up the paper and resumed reading without saying anything else. I should have known there wasn't going to be a positive word coming from his pie hole. Yeah, I was twice his size, but it still felt good to have fought back. Heck, I was bigger than most kids my age, so I guess I should have never lost a fight.

I grabbed a change of clothes, took a shower and then went into the kitchen to fix myself the customary peanut butter and jelly sandwich as well as poured a glass of milk. My mother usually spent every waking hour in the kitchen herself, while also cooking, washing dishes or doing laundry. She normally sat at the table drinking coffee and snacking on crackers, away from my father.

We sat at the table that night and talked about life in general while I ate my sandwiches. Conversations with my mother were always pleasant and uplifting; she never had anything negative to say. I think to a degree, she held a lot of things in also. I could tell that she wasn't happy, but still, she always lifted my spirits.

Wendy was coming of age and had a few neighborhood friends, so she would normally get home at night, all sweaty and dirty from playing. When not sucking up to Richard, my brother spent almost all of his time lying on the floor in front of the tube. He liked playing with little toy cars and rolling them across the floor while sucking his thumb as he looked at television.

After eating, I went to bed that night feeling pretty good about myself and therefore slept like a baby. The next day, probably around noon, Willie came to see me.

"Mike man, you messed Stacy up man. That dude got a black eye."

"Uh-uh. You're lying."

"Mike man, I ain't lying dude; you messed him up man."

I didn't believe him, so we went and snuck up behind Stacy's house while hiding behind some trees to get a glimpse of him.

He was shooting hoops by himself and by the way, Stacy was a really good basketball player. When he turned around to get a rebound, I saw his face. Yeah, I had laid it on him pretty good. He looked like a raccoon with not one, but two black eyes.

From that day on, I was tested by seemingly every kid in the neighborhood. Over the course of the following months, I fought Donald, Dick, Harry and Tommy. All of them were black kids and all smaller than me with the exception of Dick, who had about thirty pounds on me. I went 2-2 as Dick and Tommy gave me thorough butt kickings.

The fight with Douglas was crazy. We were outside one day and I don't remember how the fight started or for that matter, how any of the other fights started, just the results.

Donald and I stood there toe to toe, when I punched him in the mouth. His lip started to bleed and once he realized I injured him, he picked up a big stick and cracked me over the head with it. The stick broke and I became dazed from the blow, but after a couple of seconds of wobbling while he and the spectators looked on, I regained my composure and came back to kick his rear-end.

While I was basking in the glory of my victory, he ran into the house and before I knew it, one of his four sisters, Panola, ran out of the home and started to run towards me.

"Mike, take off man! She's coming after you!" Willie said.

Always in awe of her beauty, I stood there for a second or two. She had on shorts and looked like the thoroughbred that she was, being a high school track star and all, when Willie yelled again.

"Mike, run, that girl got a brick in her hand."

It was only at that point when I realized that I had better take off, and did. It was a good thing I had a hundred foot head start, because I would need every inch of it while running from the speedster. In a sick and demented sort of way, I thought it was kind of sexy. I finally had a girl chasing me.

She was beautiful and had those light-brown, hazel-like eyes, so I guess

I had always liked her, but because she was older than me, mature beyond her years, and mainly, because Donald and I were enemies, a mere thought of friendship was all that ever existed.

They were a very tight-knit family and very protective of their little brother and didn't take kindly to him being beat up, so I understand why Panola did what she did. She was defending her sibling.

After arriving home and into the house, all sweaty and gasping for breath, my father spoke.

"What is going on?"

"I just got into a fight with Donald and his sister picked up a brick and chased me home."

"Where is she at?"

"She is standing on the street in front of the house."

"You're running from a girl?"

"Dad, she had a brick in her hand." *a*s I was still trying to catch my breath.

With nothing more than his boxer shorts on and his gut looking as if he had swallowed a watermelon, my father stepped outside into the front yard while a whole slew of kids had formed on the street, before our home. I don't think I had been more embarrassed as a kid than that very day.

"*You got a problem?"* my father said.

'*I'm going to beat up your son."* replied Panola.

"*You touch my son and you'll pay for it with your life. Now get the hell away from my house, you bunch of Vultures!"*

The crowd then slowly dispersed.

Even though a female ran me back into my own house, it was after that fight when I finally started to get respect around the neighborhood. Nobody, not even Landry, ever bothered or picked on me again. I had also been lifting weights and was converting the so-called baby fat into muscle while turning my body into somewhat of a physique.

Thanks to me being picked on and called names by other kids, I had a lot of complexes while growing up, but had always been complimented on my looks by girls and grown-ups alike. However, I still felt like something was wrong with me.

Outside of my weight and multiple battle scars, another complex I had was my calves; I hated them. I thought they were too big and very ugly.

"*Why are my calves so big? They are ugly."* I asked my mother.

"*No they aren't, they are very shapely, muscular and sexy."*

"*There is nothing sexy about my legs; look at all of the scars."*

Michael Cavicante

"Trust me, I'm a woman, so when I say your legs are sexy, they are sexy. Women don't care about scars."

I thought she was crazy and didn't know what she was talking about. What she did know was that she wanted me circumcised. She was starting to get closer to God and had read in the Bible that all men should be circumcised. Can you believe that at the age of fourteen, I was about to undergo a procedure that I should have had at birth? I didn't know the pain I would endure after the surgery, but I quickly found out.

For those of you who may not know, circumcision is the removal of the foreskin that covers the head of the penis. Studies have shown that circumcised men are less likely to catch certain types of venereal diseases.

I was admitted to the hospital, put under sedation and after awakening, I was in the worst pain I had ever felt in my life, but was discharged and sent home.

Stitches were in my penis and hurt like the dickens. It hurt to urinate, to bathe, to sleep, and to walk; it just hurt period!! There was swelling that made it worse, but eventually, after two to four weeks, the pain went away, the stitches fell out, and I was finally back to normal; Whew!!!

Chapter 9
Freshman Year

It was autumn, 1980 and time for me to start my Freshman Year of high school and I was back at Oakhaven after a one-year absence. I had worked the summer and was able to buy some good sneakers. No, they weren't Nikes, but they were nice just the same. I was also able to buy myself some decent slacks and shirts. It felt really good to go to school dressed smartly for the first time and not wearing hand-me-downs or rags from Goodwill.

OAKHAVEN HIGH SCHOOL

Michael Cavicante

I sat in my homeroom class and observed the other students in the room. I laid eyes on a young lady by the name of Patria. She was a light-skinned, black girl with green eyes; she was gorgeous. Of course, just as always, I never said anything to her, I just observed while other guys flirted with her. I didn't know how to flirt, didn't know what to say and didn't know what to do; I just looked.

Homeroom lasted only fifteen minutes and then the bell for first period would ring. I would learn throughout the day that Patria took no other classes with me, so Homeroom was the only time I would see her. I guess you can tell that I had a crush on her.

As you can probably tell, I had a lot of crushes growing up. I was definitely girl crazy and besides, I guess I just came across a lot of pretty girls. I was just looking for one beautiful girl to befriend; that's all. I was still confused about sex and my father only confused me more; friendship is all I wanted. I was still trying to deal with what he had done to me in my own little way.

While trying to deal with my own personal problems, I noticed how many kids were driving to school. I then got the urge to want to drive, but didn't know how. Instead of confronting my dad, I figured I would teach myself, so I came up with a plan.

I waited until the family went to sleep and at two in the morning, on various days, usually on a Friday or Saturday, I snuck downstairs, found the keys to the car and took it out.

The family car was still the 1974 Pontiac Bonneville which was powered by a big V-8 engine. My father made it easy to get the car out of the driveway because he always backed in. The first couple of times were uncomfortable as I started the car, put it in gear and slowly pulled out of the driveway while trying to clear the deep ditches on each side. After finally doing so, I drove to the interstate, which was just outside the neighborhood and got on it while heading south.

All of a sudden, I was cruising at around forty miles per hour and there was little to no traffic on the roads. After about ten minutes, I exited the freeway, found my way back to Elvis Presley Boulevard and headed north back towards Norris Road. I was a natural, but drove with two feet, one on the brake and one on the accelerator which of course wasn't proper.

I normally kept the car out for about thirty minutes and returned home. The hardest part was getting it back into the driveway because of those deep ditches on each side while entering the driveway. My other problem was also trying to park it the exact same way that my dad had it parked.

A Father's Double Life

It was tough trying to back that big car in, but I managed. It must have taken me five or six tries each time while putting the car in reverse, back in drive and so on, until I finally cleared those ditches. After several times though, I mastered the art of backing in.

I must have taken the car out about ten times over the course of the next several months and couldn't believe that I hadn't been caught yet. I had the freedom of the roads, taught myself how to signal, park, change lanes smoothly, decelerate and brake properly, but was still driving with two feet. It probably would have continued for a lot longer, if not for one night in January of 1981, Robin happened to awake. I was about to pull out the driveway when he came outside.

"What are you doing Michael?
"I taught myself how to drive."
"Uh-uh, no you haven't."
"Do you want to come with me?"
"Okay."
"Well, get in."
Robin was very excited, while buckling his seat belt.
"How long have you been doing this?"
"For a little while now."
"Dang, I wish I were you."
"Why?"
"I'm not brave enough to do something like this."
"Well Robin, don't ever wish you were somebody else; you hear me?"
"Okay."
"You love who you are and never wish to be anybody else, okay?"
"Okay baby brother," he laughed.

After my lecture, I got on the interstate and punched the gas. Within seconds, we were doing well over a hundred mph; I guess I was trying to impress him. He then put his head out the window and screamed to the top of his lungs.

"SSSTTOPPP!!"
"Shut up," I said, while slowing down.
"I'm going tell dad. I'm going to tell dad."
"No you're not, because you're an accomplice, so you will be in trouble too."

I don't know where that word came from because I had never used it before. I guess I watched a lot of Beretta and Starsky & Hutch at the time, or it could have been "The Dukes of Hazzard" which was another favorite of ours. In any case, the word just came out.

We were pretty silent on the way back home while not saying much at all. I backed the car in on the first try and after turning the ignition off, I told Robin,

"You better not tell on me."

"Okay." he said.

We went into the house and got into our beds; it was around four-thirty in the morning. Later that morning, around eleven, I woke up and went over Richard's house to shoot basketball with Willie and some other neighborhood kids which was my routine on Saturday mornings. That's right, we played basketball year round and winter was no exception.

After hours of playing ball and around five in the afternoon, I went home. I walked in the door while sweaty and tired. My dad was sitting down reading the newspaper and Robin was lying on the floor in front of the television as usual; my mother was in the kitchen. While I shut and locked the door behind me, my father asked,

"So, how did you enjoy your little ride last night?"

"What are you talking about?"

"Don't lie to me, because you are only going to make matters worse."

I then realized that Robin had told on me as I said to him,

"You snitch; I'm going to get you!"

"But before you get him, I'm going to get you!" my dad replied.

I tried to get back out the door, but panicked and was unable to before my dad picked up the coffee table and threw it across the room, barely missing me.

I ran upstairs and hid under Robin's bed. Big mistake as the smell of urine suffocated me, but there was no hiding place that could have saved me and no broom this time to be poked at me. I heard his footsteps as they struck each, squeaky step on the way up, knowing that he would easily locate me. My feet were sticking out from underneath the bed.

He turned that bed over on me as slats and railings went flying through the air. If I thought the East Trigg beatings were awful, it wouldn't even come close to the ass-whipping that I was about to receive. The only difference this time was that I was a lot bigger, weighing all of two hundred ten pounds and standing just shy of six feet, so it wasn't easy for him, but my dad was very strong and he hit me with everything and anything he could find.

He started with a belt and as he swung it, I blocked it with my hand and was able to grab it away from him, but only after he hit me several times. He then took a wooden slat and started hitting me with it, but I got that away from him also, so he pulled an extension cord out of a nearby wall socket and wailed away at me with that.

If you have never been whipped with an extension cord, then trust me, you don't want to. It was the worse pain and he got at least five or six lashes across my hide. I tried to grab it, but it was too thin for me to hang on to, and the one time I did get hold of it, it burned my hands on his recoil. It was my first beating since the East Trigg slaughter, but it was the worst, longest and last beating I would ever receive at the hands of my father.

When he got done, I stayed upstairs the rest of the evening and moped. My mother came upstairs and talked to me and told me the dangers of what I had done. She also stood behind my father and the discipline that he had bestowed upon me. I fell asleep that night, woke up the next day and everything was back to normal, except for the fresh welts on my arms and legs from that extension cord.

In today's day and age, my father would have already been long since thrown in jail, but back in the day, that was just how things were. Parents and guardians could molest kids and/or get their butts whipped unmercifully and there was nothing that anybody outside of the household could do about it, or was there?

My father lectured me and asked me how long I had been doing it. I told him and he told me not to do it again as I replied,

"Yes Sir."

It was only days later when he would let me drive in the neighborhood, but only with him in the car. Despite my belief that I could drive on the main streets, it was a start. After a little while, I gained his confidence and he would let me drive by myself to the gas station to get milk, bread, etc., which was only four or five blocks away, even though I was only fourteen and too young for a driver's license. Was my father just trying to be nice, or was that his way of trying to manipulate me?

Chapter 10
Lesson Not Learned

It was late January 1981 and only days removed from my last beating. What happened to Christmas you ask? I told you in the beginning of this story that there weren't a lot of Christmas' to remember, so don't act surprised☺ Now that I have given you a reminder, back to the story.

A new President had been elected a couple months prior and was taking his oath of office on inauguration day, January twentieth; his name was Ronald Reagan. He had previously been a movie star and also served as the Governor of California. Hmmm… sounds like the exact same path someone else has taken.

The trucking company my dad had been working for went out of business, so he was unemployed. We weren't doing great financially before then, but it was enough to keep food on the table and rent paid.

He was now home more than ever and every chance he got he was talking to me about sex. I guess you wonder where my mother was during these conversations. Well, he usually talked to me when she left the house. Vanessa and mom were always going somewhere, normally on the weekends. He even went so far as to ask me,

"Do you want to have sex with your mother?"

"No." I said emphatically, but thought to myself,

"What in the world is wrong with this man?"

He also continued to talk to me about girls. You would have thought he had learned his lesson after I was admitted to Mid-South Hospital, but he obviously hadn't. He now had new tricks up his sleeve.

There was that all-important common closet mentioned earlier which connected my sister's room to my parent's room. Well, he came upstairs to visit me late one night, just days after Ronnie and Nancy made the White House their new home.

"Hey Michael," he said, as I was about to go to sleep.

"Yes dad?" I replied, while wondering what he was up to.

He sat on the edge of my bed while looking at me,

"I want you to watch your mother and I have sex."

"Why?"

"You need to see what it's like."

"But I don't want to watch you and mom have sex."

"Listen, she won't know. I drilled a hole in our closet door and placed a stool there."

"Do I have to?"

"Yes, so get up and go into Wendy's room and through her end of the closet and sit and watch, okay?"

"Okay dad."

As he headed back downstairs, I put on my robe and then followed. With my siblings asleep, I entered Wendy's room quietly and then into the closet. I ducked, bobbed, and weaved through the hanging clothes. I bet you thought I was fighting again, huh? I located the stool and then sat down. I then peeked through the hole my father drilled and soon thereafter, witnessed sexual relations between my parents. I watched for about five minutes and then became disturbed to the point that I started crying while also shaking my head in disbelief.

I got up and rushed through the hanging clothes, out of the closet and up to my room. My mother obviously heard the ruckus and came upstairs after she had put a robe on. As she came to my room, I was hysterical.

"What is wrong?" she asked, but I told her nothing. She then asked me again,

"What's wrong Michael? Why are you crying? Talk to me."

"Noth… noth… nothing Mom, I'm okay," I muttered, while hyperventilating and remaining in that state for a while.

"If you were okay, you wouldn't be crying, now what's wrong?" She then grabbed me by the shoulders and shook me while I sobbed pitifully.

"Da… da… dad…."

"Dad, what? What did dad do?"

"He… he… he."

"He what? What did dad do?"

Robin then woke up, walked over and asked,
"What's going on?"
As Robin stood there, he put his hand on my shoulder and asked,
"What's wrong little brother" and then my mother chimed in,
"Dammit Michael, tell me what's wrong. What did your father do?"
"He... he..."
"He what?"
"He...he.... he... molested me."
"When?"
"Whe... whe... when you were in the hospital"
"He didn't."
"Yes he did." As I my face flooded with tears.
"How many times?"
"Twice."
"What did he do? Did he penetrate you?"
"N...n...no."
"What did he do?"
"He...he...he...performed oral sex on me."
"Are you being honest with me son?"
"Yes mom."
Robin then said,
"Man, that's messed up; dad's a homo."
"Shut up Robin!" she said.
"Well what happened tonight? What caused you to start crying tonight?"
"He...he...he drilled a hole in your closet door and wanted me to watch you and him have sex."
"He did what?"
"I was sitting in your closet watching dad and you have sex, but couldn't stand to watch anymore. That's when I ran out of the closet and upstairs."
"That's the noise I heard, you were in the closet?"
"Yes mom, I was in the closet."
"I'm going to kill him…..I am going to kill him." she replied.
Robin then responded,
"Yeah ma, go kill him mom. Let's get him." As Robin grabbed his crotch with one hand and bit his other wrist. That is what he did when he got over-exuberant.
"Robin, stop it; I didn't mean it literally."

"Are you going to be okay son?"
"I'm going to be okay."
"Are you sure?"
"Yes mother."
"I'm so sorry baby, I'm so sorry," as she kissed me and held me in her arms.

She made sure I was okay and then went downstairs. World War III soon broke out as I heard my parents yelling and screaming.

Shortly thereafter, I heard Wendy crying. I wanted to go downstairs and console my little sister but was afraid, so I just sat in my room and cried. Robin stayed by my side trying to console me while offering a hug or two.

"Dad really did that to you?"
"Yes Robin, he did."
"Why didn't you tell me?"
"I didn't want to tell anybody."
"I'm sorry little brother, everything is going to be okay."
"Thanks Robin."

MY FATHER IS STANDING ON A MILK CRATE TO APPEAR TALLER THAN MY MOTHER IN THIS 1980'S PHOTO.

Robin then went and lied on his bed while I cried myself to sleep as the screaming and yelling finally subsided.

I woke up the next morning, went downstairs and saw my mother sleeping on the couch. I later in life figured out that it should have been the other way around. She awakened, saw me and asked if I was okay, at which point I told her yes. She asked me to come to her and I did. She sat up on the couch, held me in her arms and apologized again for what my father had done. It was a Saturday morning and a very awkward one as my father woke up. I don't think they spoke to each other for a month.

In the meantime, my mother took immediate action. One day, I came home from school and met Ms. Patton, who was from the Dept. of Social Services.

She was a black woman, slender, well dressed, nice looking, very articulate and extremely professional. She sat down with my parents and me while talking to us. She explained what would be happening in the weeks/months to come and that there would be in-home counseling sessions twice a week.

While attending counseling sessions at home, I was still trying to live my life as a child, away from the home. I went out for the Varsity football team during spring training. It started in mid-February and David was the head coach.

I was already close to six feet tall and over two hundred pounds and within the last six months, had transformed my body, even more, into a muscular physique from weightlifting. I was big boned and had the genetic make-up to build muscle mass fast. I was even the talk of the weight-room as just before my fifteenth birthday I was already bench-pressing three hundred pounds and leg pressing well over six hundred; I was a beast.

David loved my size and after watching me play catch with another player, he decided to try me out at tight end. The Quarterback started throwing me balls and I was catching everything thrown to me. If it touched my fingertips, I was catching it.

There was one ball thrown to me that was like a laser coming from the signal caller's arm. I had run a twenty-yard in-route when the ball came whistling in, thrown low to the ground, but I dived and caught it. It was only an inch from touching the turf, but never did as I snagged it, rolled over and back onto my feet; I was totally pumped while other players clapped. It was at that point when Coach David made the statement.

"I think we have found our next starting tight-end."

"Really, are you serious?" I exclaimed.

Michael Cavicante

"*Hell yeah, who knows, you might take Frog's job next year.*"

Frog was Cornelius' nickname and he was a great tight end, receiving honorable mention the previous season, so I didn't think that I would be replacing him, at least not just yet. Coach just said that to get under his skin as Frog looked at me with kind of a smirk.

That didn't stop me from being excited. I was the first one to spring training every day. I ran flag and post routes while someone threw me the ball; I never dropped a pass. My mother was against me playing football because she was afraid I would get hurt again, but she supported me nonetheless.

Shortly thereafter and during the school day, even though I was excited about what I was doing on the football field, I was telling stories to my fellow classmates of how I taught myself to drive. They were amazed at my story as I described to them how I took the car in the middle of the night while my parents slept, when all of a sudden I was paged to the office.

I told my fellow classmates and friends that I would see them later while not having a clue as to why I was being called to the office.

It was a mid-March morning, less than two weeks removed from my fifteenth birthday, when I got to the office and Ms. Patton was standing there with Robin waiting on me. It was only eight-fifteen and the school day had barely got started.

"*Where are we going?* I asked.
"*We have to go to court.*" She replied.
"*Why do we have to go there?*"
"*We will find out when we get there? Okay?*"
"*Okay.*"

After checking us out of school, we walked to her car and then headed to the courthouse.

After a twenty-minute ride to downtown Memphis, we got out of the car, entered the building and headed to the courtroom area. The corridor was full of people; some were standing, some sitting. I saw my parents sitting in the hallway with my sister Wendy in close proximity. None of us were really talking to each other; we just waited patiently until we were called before the judge.

Why were we there? And what was about to happen to us?

Chapter 11
A Mother's Devastation

It was a beautiful day in March, only days away from the first day of spring, when the time had come for Ms. Patton to escort all of us into the courtroom. We took our seats as the case was announced. Afterwards, the Judge read the documents handed to him by Ms. Patton and minutes later rendered his verdict, based on the information that was provided to him.

The Judge then stated,

"I hereby remove Robin, Michael, and Wendy Cavicante, from the custody of Raymond and Juanita Cavicante for a time that will be later determined, but only after Raymond Cavicante has sought and undergone Psychiatric Evaluation."

"What does that mean? Where are we going?" I responded, while my siblings and I were whisked away by Social Service Authorities.

"What's going on? What's happening? Mom, where are they taking us?" I screamed, while looking in my mother's direction.

My mother was yelling at my father,

"I hate you! They took my kids away. I hate you!" she shouted, as she had to be restrained and escorted out of courtroom.

Tears came to my eyes as I write this part of the story as they did when I wrote while explaining earlier what my father had done to me. I guess it will never escape me.

As we were moved further away from my mother's presence, her voice faded away, along with the sight of her. When would we ever see her again?

We were all sent to shelters. My baby sister was sent to a Foster Home in North Memphis off of Chelsea Avenue. Because Wendy was a pre-teen, she was able to stay in one place for the period of time that we were out of our home.

For my brother and me, it was a different story since we were teenagers. We would be transferred from place to place to place. Our first stop was Porter Leath Children's Center, which was also in North Memphis, but on Manassas. It was a temporary holding center for kids until the city could find permanent placement. I guess you could say that like a distressed airplane, we were in a holding pattern.

It resembled a big two-story house, but also served as an office building due to counselors also working there. Downstairs, there was a lounge, dining room, kitchen, and bathroom, along with some offices. The normal stay was supposed to be thirty days.

It was during the stay at Porter Leath that I met Rosie. She was a red headed, white girl that must have had freckles on every part of her body and was absolutely crazy about me. She was sixteen years old.

I guess the opposite sex really liked me, but my father had turned me off about girls and sex. Yes, I wanted a female friend, but other than that, I didn't know anything about sex and didn't want to know anything about it. She must have thought I was gay, because she tried to kiss me on the lips at times and I would turn my head. Rosie followed me everywhere I went within the complex. I must admit that I enjoyed the attention.

I was enrolled at Humes Junior High, right down the street, to finish my ninth grade year. It was the same school that Elvis Presley went to as a child. I didn't know it at the time, but it's not like it would have been a big deal; I just wanted to give you a little trivia. It wasn't until years later when I saw his life story that I realized I too had gone there.

At Humes, my next crush was Tamara; she was gorgeous. She had flawless, brown skin, the cutest smile, was slender and very smart. She also had a beauty mole on her face. I guess I had a subconscious thing about moles.

There was another very pretty girl whose name was Linda and who was also beautiful. She was of light complexion and very sweet. She once gave me a manicure in Health Class. I guess hygiene was part of the curriculum.

Yes, I was definitely at the age where I liked girls, but looking at them was good enough for me. I wanted no part of intimacy, so when I say crush, it just meant that I was enamored by their beauty. All of this was short-lived and my freshman year quickly came to an end as we closed out the month of May.

Back at Porter Leath, Robin and I got word that we were to be transferred somewhere else. When Rosie found out, I guess she wanted to say her good-byes, so one night she snuck over to my room via the roof as the sleeping quarters were upstairs.

The boy's and girl's rooms were separated by a single, dead-bolted, locked door at night, after hours, so Rosie left her room through an upstairs window, walked across the rooftop, came to my room and knocked on the window. After being startled, I opened it for her.

"What are you doing?"

"I came to say my good-byes."

She then started kissing me and tried to hold me, but I pushed her away.

"What's wrong with you?" she asked.

"Nothing, I just…"

"Hey Rosie, he don't know what to do. Come over to my room." Another guy, Steven, had stepped into my doorway.

To my surprise, Rosie left me and joined him, while I lay back down.

After a little while, he came out of his room and had blood all over his lower body. I thought that he had killed her.

"What happened?" I asked.

"Man, she's on her damn period!" Steven replied.

"What does that mean?"

He just shook his head at me and then went to wash up. I went into his room and there was blood all over his sheets.

"Where is Rosie?' What did you do to her?"

"She went out of the window and back to her room Mike."

"Is she okay? There is a lot of blood on your sheets."

"Yeah Mike, now go to bed."

While lying in bed, I was confused and tossed and turned all night, while hoping that Rosie was okay and thinking to myself,

"Why was she bleeding so badly? What did he do to her?"

The next morning after seeing Rosie and finally relieved, I helped Steven get the bloody sheets downstairs. I don't remember how we did it, but we managed to get them past the house parent and into the laundry room. I then grabbed some clean sheets, snuck them upstairs and helped remake his bed. A few minutes later while back downstairs, I saw Rosie again.

"Are you okay?"

"I'm fine Michael, why do you ask?"

"I saw all of this blood on Steven's sheets; I thought something had happened to you."

"I'm fine Michael, I just got my period."

"Yeah, that's the same thing Steven told me, but I don't understand it."

"All you need to know is that it is perfectly normal and happens with all females once a month, and can last anywhere from three to seven days. I'm not a doctor and therefore can't articulate its exact meaning, but it is perfectly normal and therefore, I am okay, okay?"

"Okay." I replied

It wasn't long after that when in late May, after school let out for the summer, when my brother and I were transferred. We had certainly stayed longer than normally allowed which equated to around seventy-five days. Our next stop was The Runaway House and as its name implied, it was a place where runaway kids could go to find counseling and solace.

The Runaway House was located in the heart of Overton Square which was a very happening district in Memphis and included plenty of eateries. There always seemed to be something going on because we often heard the sound of music, live bands and witnessed the hustle and bustle of the area. However, we weren't allowed to leave the confines of the Runaway House, except when we were taken somewhere by one of the house parents.

Robin and I weren't runaways, but I probably should've run away long before everything happened.

My brother and I were the only black kids there; however, none of the white kids thought I was black. At the age of fifteen, I still had my California dialect and liked rock music. To this day, people that don't know me think I am either Mexican, Latino, or of some other Hispanic descent. I guess I am to a degree, since my father was of Italian descent, but still, I considered myself an African-American.

The Runaway House was another pretty, big house. As you walked in the front door, there was an office to the right and as you continued to walk through, you would run into the lounge area where the residents spent most of the day; it also accessed the upstairs, which is where the girls slept. You then walked into the kitchen and to the right of the kitchen was a hallway. In that hallway and to the right was the boy's bedroom. It had four sets of bunk beds situated very close together. There were also two windows that usually stayed open and at night, a nice breeze often cooled the room, not to mention, allowed us to hear live music playing from nearby venues.

Across the hallway from the bedroom was the office that the counselors used during the workday. The counselors were, Michael, who was a lean, tall, blonde-haired, white guy who wore these thin-rimmed, wire glasses. He resembled John Lennon, with the exception of the blonde hair of course.

My other counselor was Olivia. She was a very nice, beautiful white lady with long black hair and often took us on little excursions, which included the movies. Olivia was also my favorite person to talk to.

She took us to see the movie *"Hardly Working"*, staring Jerry Lewis, which at the time, was only the second movie that I had ever seen in a theatre. The movie was hilarious and I had been a Jerry Lewis fan long before then, so for me, it was quite a treat.

The counselors normally left and went home around five in the afternoon. Marcy, the overnight house parent normally showed up around four thirty.

Like my father—Marcy was of Italian decent, and like my father, she had jet black, wavy and curly hair. She often wore dresses and skirts, that exposed her hairy legs and when I say hairy—I mean they were really hairy. I would learn later that it was customary for Italian women not to shave their legs.

I experienced a lot at the Runaway House while Robin and I spent the whole summer there. The kids there loved me, as did most who met me, but white kids especially liked me. I think I related better to them for whatever reason, or was it that I was just gullible?

The most memorable event while at The Runaway House happened on a mid-August, summer night. We were outside in the backyard playing basketball when one of the boys approached me.

"Hey Michael, Marcy has a bag of Oregano in her purse, can you go get it?"

"Sure." I replied.

I wanted so badly to be accepted and therefore did almost anything that was asked of me by my peers, so I went into the house and found her purse. She was taking a nap at the time, but I saw her bag sitting close by and saw the big plastic bag of Oregano sitting near the top. I quietly and slowly worked my way to it, grabbed it and then ran outside.

I know you probably think I was dumb by some of the things that I did as a kid. I wasn't, just very naïve as to the ways of the world. Anyway,

I took the bag outside and gave it to my friend, Danny. He then sat on top of the dumpster, poured the bag of spice onto a newspaper and began sifting through it. While curious, I asked him,

"What are you doing?"

"I'm separating the seeds from the oregano," he laughed.

I continued to shoot basketball with the other runaways, but continued to observe what Danny was doing. I then saw him put the oregano in some paper, roll it up, lick it and then fire it up with a lighter. I then saw him smoking the oregano and thought to myself,

"Why is he smoking a condiment?"

After finishing it, he must have rolled about twenty more cigarettes full of oregano. Afterwards, he and the rest of the Runaways started smoking while I continued to shoot basketball by myself and watched them puff away.

"Hey Michael, do you want to smoke with us?"

"Nah, I don't smoke cigarettes."

"It's not a cigarette; it's a healing aide."

"But there ain't nothing wrong with me."

"It will make you feel better anyway."

"Okay, I guess."

After dropping the basketball, I walked over to the dumpster where the residents were assembled and they handed me a lit cigarette.

"Go ahead Michael and hit it." I then swatted it out of my hand.

"Not hit it-hit it." as they laughed ridiculously at me.

"Hit it means to take a drag."

"Oh." I replied.

After picking up the doobie and re-lightening it for me while continuing to laugh, I took a drag while holding it like a cigarette.

"No Mike, you have to hold it like this".

So I took my thumb and index finger and held the end of the blunt while taking a big drag. I felt light-headed all of a sudden, but at the same time, it felt pretty good. I took another toke and another and then another.

"Damn Mike, slow down bro!" and as they laughed, I was getting high as a kite.

They showed me how to receive shotguns. Danny took the lit end of the joint, stuck it in his mouth and blew smoke out of the other end while I put both hands up to my face in order to direct the smoke into my nostrils; man how my nose burned. They then had me blow them shotguns; I was quickly a pro. We must have smoked all those joints that night as I finally realized from previous hearsay that what we were really smoking wasn't oregano, but marijuana.

I had heard about it, but until that night, never saw it, touched it or smelled it. Yeah, kind of like a vagina as far as I was concerned; I had never seen one, touched one, or smelled one. We were outside until like two in the morning when finally we went into the house.

With my mouth dry and pasty, head swimming and literally feeling on cloud nine, I felt great. Yeah, I enjoyed the feeling. I found a bag of Doritos to munch on and then went and lay on the sofa. After eating the bag of Doritos, I got up and went into kitchen looking for something else to eat and couldn't understand why I seemingly couldn't get enough to grub on.

"What's wrong with me?" I said loudly.

"You got what's called, the motha-fuckin' munchies dude." Danny exclaimed, and laughed.

I finally found and popped some popcorn and then went back into the den where all of us were watching the new phenomena that had just hit the television airwaves and that was MTV; Comments were made by virtually everyone in the room.

"Man, this fuckin' MTV is far out."

"Yeah, like totally rad man."

"This is some psychedelic shit; all I need are some 'ludes and I will be straight."

"Whoever invented this shit is going to be rich."

"Man, that music is fuckin' rockin'."

"Fuckin' videos to go with the music, now that's the shit."

"Man that chick is hot."

It was obvious that MTV had taken us all by storm and as we turned up the sound while listening to the music and looking at the videos, it must have awakened the sleeping Marcy, because all of a sudden, she stormed into the room, turned down the volume and was standing over me while looking me dead in the eyes.

I guess she came directly to me because I was the honest one of the bunch. All of us were in the same room, the lounge I guess you would call it. We were all sprawled out on beanbags, sofas, and chairs, watching the boob tube when she asked,

"Michael; who took the plastic bag out of my purse?"

I didn't say a word at first, because even though high as a kite, I was rationalizing the whole situation. I realized that she was an employee of the Runaway House and probably shouldn't have brought the marijuana onto the premises in the first place. After a few seconds elapsed, she then asked me again,

"Michael; who took that bag out of my purse?"

"Arrrreee yoouuu talllkking about the maarijuana?" I stammered, as my speech became long and drawn out.

"Yes Michael!"

"I took it. And what the fuck are you going to do about it bitch?"

I was as high as a kite and it was clearly, my **BRAIN ON DRUGS**, because that was not Michael Cavicante talking.

It was safe to say that my innocence was slowly slipping away. Up to that day in my life, I had never so much as cursed, called anyone a name and certainly had never disrespected anyone, especially an adult, but all of a sudden and in one sentence, I had done all three.

She was pissed off while standing over me for a second or two and was speechless while glaring into my dilated pupils while I stared back at her with a big smile on my face. She had a look of disbelief on her face, not only because we had smoked her weed, but also because the sweet, innocent and honest boy, whom she had come to know, wasn't so sweet and innocent anymore, but honest I still was.

I guess she also realized that there was in fact, nothing that she could do about it and Marcy stormed out of the room while we all laughed out loudly.

Yeah, I must say my first marijuana experience was fun, but I realized it was wrong and vowed never smoke again. I had been taught at a young age that marijuana burns out your brain cells, but still didn't understand how something that made you feel so good, could be so bad for you. I feel your pain Ricky Williams.

Chapter 12

Back to Court

A COUPLE OF WEEKS AFTER MY marijuana experiment, in late August, 1981, me and my siblings found our way back into court. No, it wasn't because of the marijuana incident, but because the judge wanted to review our case and decide whether or not my siblings and I should be allowed to go back home. I was excited because I just knew that we were going to be reunited with our parents. I hadn't seen them in about six months and also had enough of being shipped around.

We were allowed no contact with them. I also hadn't spoken to my sister since we separated and was missing her a lot. After everything my dad had put the family through, I still loved him and wanted badly to have a healthy relationship with him.

We entered the courtroom, and afterwards, the Judge read some paperwork handed to him. Upon his completion, he decided to keep us away from our parents a bit longer. I didn't cry, because like the physical pain I had become accustomed to, I had also become immune to the whole situation.

Wendy remained in the custody of the foster parents she was originally sent to, and Robin and I were sent to Dogwood Village, in Eads, Tennessee, about thirty miles away from our home on West Ball.

I hadn't a clue as to what Wendy was thinking through all of this. She didn't know why we weren't living at home and therefore wasn't aware of what our dad had done to me. During the court proceedings, she didn't seem upset or sad and actually seemed pretty upbeat and happy. As far as

Michael Cavicante

Robin and me, we arrived at Dogwood Village in late August, just in time for my tenth grade year. That's right; I was somehow miraculously passing school and enrolled at Collierville High, home of the Dragons.

All I recall about the school is that they had an awesome football team that year, because I do know that they were undefeated, with a 10-0 record at one point. I wanted to play, but wasn't permitted to, due to the restrictions placed on us at Dogwood. That is all I remember about Collierville High.

Dogwood Village consisted of five ranch style brick houses that were called cottages and numbered one through five. Each cottage had four bedrooms, a family room, kitchen, dining room and two bathrooms.

Each home accommodated anywhere from four to six youths, plus the house parents. There were two cottages for the girls and three for the boys. I lived in the second cottage from the main road (cottage number two), which was HWY 64. My brother was in the third cottage (cottage number three) right next door to me. I hadn't a clue as to why they would separate brothers.

Our house parents were Mr. and Mrs. Frye. They were an older, married, white couple in their sixties, I would say. They were nice, but stern; I guess they had to be.

In my cottage, there were five of us. The boys I remember were Jerome and Charlie. You will find out soon as to why I remember those names in particular.

I didn't like Collierville High School, so I went to class and didn't talk to anybody, or was it that I had just become sort of a loaner and therefore reclusive? Back at Dogwood, everyday was the same routine, nothing exciting and nothing new. Bedtime was nine o'clock sharp and we were awakened at five-thirty.

One day after school, all of the boys and girls from each of the five cottages met outside for recreation; guess who I saw? It was Rosie, the red headed, freckle-faced, white girl I met at Porter Leath. Although I wasn't crazy about her, it was nice to see a familiar face. We talked for a while and shared our experiences over the last several months, but other than a few words, that was about it.

It seemed as if trouble always seemed to find me. I had been at Dogwood for a little over two months when on an early November night, lights went out at nine as usual, but on that particular Thursday night, something was about to happen. It seemed like everyone in the cottage knew what was going on except me.

A Father's Double Life

While lying in my bed unable to sleep, I saw Jerome walk by my room around midnight. My bedroom just so happened to be the closest to the back door when I heard it open and then saw female silhouettes pass by.

I then jumped out of bed and walked to the doorway, peaked out and saw girls walking down the hallway giggling. While looking back to my right, the next girl to enter was Rosie. The girls from cottage one had invaded our quarters.

"*What are you doing here?*" I asked.

"*I'm here to see you,*" she replied, as she pushed me out of the doorway and into the room.

I knew I liked girls, but wasn't ready for something like that. I felt my heart palpitating while she led me to the bed. I knew that I wasn't ready for intimacy, but Rosie left me with very few options and this time she wasn't going to take no for an answer. She wanted me and wanted me badly, so on that night, I reluctantly let her have her way.

She led me to the bed and fell on top of me as we landed on the soft mattress. While straddling me, she started kissing me and simultaneously pulling my underwear down. I knew enough to pull my t-shirt up and off of my body. I got excited and could hardly breathe as she was soon totally naked.

A girl had never been that close to me, not a naked one anyway. I didn't know what to do, but I soon felt her soft nipples graze my chest. She then put one of them in my mouth and told me to suck on it, so I did while shivering as if it were ten degrees in the room. While she started to moan and groan, my body shook as she gently kissed my face.

She then took her hand and grabbed my penis. I didn't know what to expect next. I had my eyes closed and was enjoying the warmth and feel of her sultry body when all of a sudden she was off of me and under the bed. I wondered what the heck was going on, but I looked out the door and saw a flashlight's ray against the floor as I pulled the covers back over me; it had to be Mr. Frye. Rosie obviously heard something that I hadn't. Mr. Frye must have been awakened by the subtle noises throughout the house.

While I played possum, he turned my light on for a few seconds and then flipped it back off. I then opened my eyes and then heard him in another room ask,

"*What the hell is going on around here?*" and it sounded so funny, with his old, crackly voice, I was laughing my ass off.

Soon thereafter, I saw girls scurry passed my room and out the back door when it slammed shut. After making sure that Mr. Frye had gone back to his room, Rosie removed herself from under my bed, got dressed and left in a hurry while saying goodnight.

I lay there in my bed while wondering if there would be any repercussions for Mr. Frye finding the girls in the house, but eventually went to sleep.

Everything seemed normal the next day as we all got up and went to school. Later that day, after the school bus dropped us off and we were back at our cottage, we were summoned by the head honcho to be at the Administration Building at four o'clock. So at three fifty-five, all of the boys in our cottage, along with Mr. Frye, took the brief walk down to the main offices to meet our fate.

After arriving, we all sat in an executive meeting room. The table was cherry wood, the chairs had leather surfaces and on the other side of the table were the girls that had invaded our cottage the night before.

Mr. Coughlin, the director, held all of us in that room and asked about the night in question.

"Who opened the door to let the girls in?" he asked.

Everyone just sat around the table and looked at each other with slight smirks on our faces. No one uttered a word as Mr. Coughlin then asked,

"Which girls actually went to Cottage number two and what exactly happened?

Which in retrospect was a pretty stupid question, especially coming from a fifty-year old man, but everyone was silent, not saying a word. His questioning went on for about fifteen minutes.

Finally, after not being able to get to the bottom of it, Mr. Coughlin placed all of us on cottage restriction, which meant outside of going to school, we weren't to leave our homes. He also made bedtime six o'clock and also took away television privileges. This punishment would be in force for thirty days. Well I must say that I had already had enough of Dogwood Village and made plans to run away with Jerome and Charlie.

Chapter 13
The Runaway

Although only fifteen years old and the youngest of the three, with Jerome being seventeen and Charlie sixteen, it was me that orchestrated the runaway from Dogwood Village. It was evident that I was a natural born leader, but hadn't realized it at that point in my life. Then again, it wasn't like there was a whole lot of thought that had to be put in to it. We just had to decide on a night to leave and where we were going.

I decided that we leave on a Friday night and since I lived the closest, we would go to my house. Since I had learned how to drive, the plan was for us to get to my home, have Jerome hot-wire the car and I was to take him and Charlie home. I didn't realize it was thirty miles away, or if I did, I didn't realize or have a concept as to how long thirty miles actually was. We just knew that my house was the closest.

The very next Friday, a week after we were placed on restriction and on an early to mid-November night, Jerome, Charlie and myself, set out on our thirty-mile journey at nine forty-five. When we got out to the main highway, we proclaimed ourselves The Three Musketeers. It was at that point when Jerome came up with the bright idea of doubling back and breaking into the Administration Building.

Charlie and I were against it and therefore told Jerome that we wanted no part of his foolishness, but he was convinced that we needed money and that he thought there would be some in the Administration Building.

Charlie and I still weren't going along with and wanted no part of Jerome's plan, so Jerome walked back onto the premises by himself while Charlie and I waited on the side of the road, just outside the main entrance.

About ten minutes passed by, when all of a sudden we heard glass break. Almost simultaneously, we heard what sounded like an alarm going off. Charlie and I started running like the dickens down the highway. I don't know exactly what a dickens is, or how fast it is, but it couldn't be any faster than we were running. It was pitch black and I don't remember any streetlights, but the moon lit the road just enough for us to be able to see where we were going. Highway 64 was a long dark stretch of pavement.

It was my idea that every time we saw a car's headlights to stop running and dive into the ditch that ran alongside the road, just in case it happened to be the police or Dogwood Village Authorities. After a car passed, we would get up and start running again.

It seemed like we were running for our lives and also running out of breath, but kept running anyway until we felt like we were safe from being caught. After about ten minutes, we stopped and rested while lying in the grass on the side of the road.

We were exhausted already and hadn't even gotten off the main highway. We lie down breathing heavily unable to even talk when suddenly we heard leaves rustling. We got scared out of our wits as we lifted our heads to look around. Low and behold, it was Jerome. He was sweating heavily and his eyes were as big as saucers as he gasped for breath.

We gave him a minute to catch his wind and then instead of asking him if he was okay, Charlie asked,

"Did you get any money?" Showed where our priorities were.

While still sucking wind, he said,

"No man. After the alarm sounded, I took off."

"Yeah we heard the window break and the alarm go off; that is when we took off running." I replied.

Jerome had to be booking it to catch up with us as fast as he did, because the Administration Building was at least sixty yards from the main entrance and Charlie and I had run at least half a mile. After giving him the chance to tell his story, we gave our friend a chance to rest. After about fifteen minutes, we got up and continued our long journey.

After traveling on Highway 64 for several more miles or so, we saw the Interstate I-40 junction, which crossed over the main road. The exchange was well lit, almost like a football stadium at night. We walked up a grassy knoll and onto the interstate and headed towards Memphis. The time was somewhere between eleven-thirty and midnight.

We walked and walked and walked some more while on the shoulder of the road. It must have been about two-thirty when I saw a sign that said Summer Avenue. I recognized the street name, so we got off of the interstate and started walking down the familiar boulevard. I thought we were close to my house, but we continued to tread some more.

We trudged along for miles and talked about what we were going to do when arriving at our individual destinations. The weather was clear, the moon was bright and a soft breeze kept us cool. As the early morning hours slowly crept by, I saw a sign that said East Parkway.

I certainly recognized Parkway. It was the East part that threw me off at which point Jerome and Charlie started doubting the fact if I really knew where we were going, or better yet, were we lost? I reassured them that we were going in the right direction, even though at that point, I wasn't so sure myself, but we continued to trek on. Until that very night, I had no idea how long Parkway really was.

We arrived at Lamar Avenue at which point I was very familiar where we were, because my father had driven through that intersection many times with me in the car.

Parkway jumped over and took on another direction and turned into South Parkway. Suddenly, it was that end of the confusing street, less than an hour later and around six in the morning when we arrived at the intersection of Elvis Presley Boulevard and South Parkway. I finally had no doubt as to where we were.

Bellevue Park, which if you remember, was the same park that I got in trouble as a younger kid when I pulled down that Fire Alarm, was located at that particular intersection. I therefore knew we didn't have far to go, as the old Trigg address and my Ball Road address weren't that far apart. The park has since been renamed, Jesse H. Turner Park.

We were less than five miles from my front door. In relation to the twenty-five miles that we had already traveled, that was nothing. I couldn't speak for Charlie or Jerome, but I was tired and my feet were killing me, but we lumbered along, finally arriving at my house at seven o'clock on Saturday morning.

We tried to jimmy the door and get into the new family car, which was a 1976 Ford Thunderbird, but were unsuccessful. Jerome wanted to break a window to get in, but I wouldn't allow it and after several failed attempts to gain access, we went to the entrance of my house; we were all very tired. I knocked on the door and my mother answered while screaming for joy.

"*My baby, my baby!*" she exclaimed as we all walked into the home.

I then introduced Jerome and Charlie as she greeted them with open arms. Not caring to eat or drink anything, nor taking showers, my buddies crashed out on the living room floor. I did take a shower, went upstairs and got into my bed. After eight plus hours of sleep, I woke up around four-thirty and went downstairs only to find two thirds of The Three Musketeers gone.

"*Where are Charlie and Jerome?*"

"*They said that they had to go and to tell you good-bye.*" my mother replied.

She also told me that she fed them. My dad's new way of earning a living was driving a cab. They were barely talking to each other and she was still being his servant while fixing his meals and waiting on him hand and foot like she had always done. He didn't deserve to be treated like a king.

My mother asked me what happened and I told her that I didn't like Dogwood Village. I told her about the chain of events leading up to the runaway. She urged me to go back and that I was only making matters worse. I told her that I didn't want to go back, but she convinced me to. My only request was could I just stay the weekend. She said, *"Okay"* so I enjoyed my weekend with her and on Monday morning I called Dogwood Village.

"*Good Morning, Dogwood Village.*"

"*Hello, this is Michael Cavicante.*"

"*Michael, where are you son?*"

"*Who is this?*"

"*Bennett, now where are you at?*"

"*If I tell you where I'm at, will you come get me?*"

"*Sure will.*"

"*Will I be taken back to Dogwood?*"

"*Absolutely, where else would we take you?*"

"*You promise?*"

'*Yes Michael, now where are you?*"

"*I'm at home with my mother.*"

"*What's that address?*"

" ***** West Ball Road, in Memphis.*"

"*Are Jerome and Charlie with you?*"

"*No sir.*"

"*Where are they at?*"

"I don't know sir. We broke up once we got to Memphis."
"Alright, we'll be right there."
"How long sir?"
"Within the next hour or so."
"Okay sir, bye."
"Wait a minute. You are you going to be there, aren't you?"
"Yes Sir."
"Alright, see you then."
"Okay."

During the next couple of hours, my mother and I sat around and talked, while my father left in his taxi. While we sat in the dining room, we noticed a car pulling into our gravel-filled driveway; it must have been Dogwood Authorities.

We walked to the door and I hugged my mother good-bye while giving her a kiss on the cheek. As she stood at the door, I walked out towards the big, shiny car that awaited my entry. A black guy got out and held the rear door open for me, but first, he put handcuffs on. He then placed his hand on my head, pushed it forward and down while guiding me into the backseat.

As he backed out of the driveway, I noticed my mother still standing in the doorway looking sad. I felt bad for her because I knew she was trapped in a situation that she didn't want to be in, but she had very few alternatives, if any. She knew that if there was any chance of seeing her kids again, she had to stay with my father, because she couldn't afford to take care of us on her own.

While I was thinking about my mother and the situation as a whole, I realized that we weren't going back to Dogwood Village after all.

"Where are we going?" I asked.
"Juvenile Hall."
"But I called Dogwood Village and was told that I would be taken back there."
"That was me you talked to."
"Well, why did you tell me I'd be taken back to Dogwood Village?"
"Because if I had told you that I was taking you to Juvenile Hall, you wouldn't have told me where you were."

I thought to myself,
"You lied to a kid? What a dirty creep."

After arriving at Juvenile hall, I was taken inside, checked in, and detained in a cell. I had seen more of that place already than I ever cared to see. The previous two times, I was held in a waiting room while my mother came to pick me up, but this time I was in an actual cell.

It wasn't a cell like you see on television with bars. It was a 5x7 room with a metal toilet and a bed attached to the wall, which was more like a metal sheet, with a flimsy, two-inch mattress on top of it. It was starting to get cold outside, especially at night, so the cell was heated through the floor.

The floor got so hot at times, I couldn't walk on it; if I did, I would literally burn my feet, so I was forced to stay in/on my bed; maybe that was their intention. The door entering the cell was made of heavy gauged steel and also had a window that was of course, unbreakable. Okay, so it might have been like a jail cell that you see on the tube, with the exception of not having bars.

During the day, we juveniles sat in a large room, watched television and played either checkers or cards. After a couple of days, I was interrogated.

"So who broke into the administration building?"

"I don't know."

"It seems like some coincidence that the administration building was broken into the same night you and your buddies ran away from Dogwood Village."

"I don't know anything about it sir."

"Is that your story?"

"Yes Sir."

"You do realize that you are going to be here until we get to the bottom of this."

"Yes sir."

"But you don't know anything about the break-in?"

"No Sir."

"Okay, well I hope you make yourself comfortable here, because you are going to be here a long time." He got up and walked out of the room.

I guess I was just going to rot in that place, because when I was a kid, you just didn't snitch. It was the golden rule amongst us; you just didn't do it. That was how I felt at that particular time anyway.

As days went by, I was interrogated several more times, but remained tight-lipped about the incident. Four weeks later, on an early December morning, I walked into the Recreation Room and to my surprise Charlie was sitting there. I walked over to him.

"Hey Charlie, how are you doing?"
"How you think I am doing? I'm in here Mike."
I thought to myself, *"Okay, stupid question."*

I don't remember how he ended up there, but we were together once more.

Charlie was also interrogated, but remained silent. About two more weeks passed by and Jerome showed up. How he got caught, I don't remember either, but shortly thereafter, the three of us were questioned together.

Nobody was talking because we were the three Musketeers. Well, I realized that we were in fact going to be there until they got to the bottom of it. Jerome must have vandalized the place, or really did find some money, if not both, and just didn't tell us about it. I just couldn't believe all of the fuss was over a broken window. After thinking the whole thing through, I went to Charlie.

"Listen Charlie, until we talk, we are going to be here. We need to tell them that Jerome broke into the building."

"But Mike, we're The Three Musketeers," as he laughed crazily.

I looked at him like he really was insane and replied,

"Man, forget some damn Three Musketeers. If we don't tell on Jerome, we are going to be here forever."

"Okay Mike, okay; I'm in."

"Are you sure?"

"Yeah Mike, let's do this so we can get the hell out of here."

"Okay."

I then asked a guard to summon the investigator, and Charlie and I dropped dime on Jerome. We didn't want to, but realized we had to do it.

Chapter 14
Verdict is in

After spending eight weeks in Juvenile Hall, which included Christmas and New Year's Eve, I went to court, along with Charlie and Jerome. Shortly thereafter, the Judge read our statements to himself and then rendered his verdict.

Because Jerome had turned eighteen, he was sent to a correctional center in Nashville, Charlie was sent back to Dogwood Village and I was sent to Porter Leath Group Home. I recognized the name when I heard it, but it was different from the first place that Robin and I had gone to; that was Porter Leath Children's Center. I eventually found out that they were both affiliated.

I didn't know what to expect while being separated from my brother for the first time as he was still at Dogwood Village. I felt bad about leaving him there, but I knew that I couldn't tell him anything about the plan to run away, because he might have told on us, just like he did when I snuck the car out. The bottom line was—I didn't trust my own brother.

It was an early to mid-January day when I was transported from the courthouse to Porter Leath. I arrived at the house that was located in North Memphis on the corner of North Parkway and Dunlap Avenue; the front facing North Parkway. I noticed how big the dwelling was when we pulled into the driveway of the all brick, two-story home.

I was escorted inside and met my houseparent, Hazel. Serving as the permanent house guardian, she was an early fifties dark-skinned, medium-build, black lady, who greeted me and showed me around.

Michael Cavicante

The house was huge. Downstairs there was a living room, recreation room with a pool table, kitchen, bathroom and Hazel's bedroom. Upstairs, there were four or five bedrooms. I had to share a room with another boy, which I didn't mind. There was an initial warmth and coziness about the home. I must say that I felt like it was the best place I had been by far.

It was strictly a boys' home, which was fine with me. Hazel was the warmest and nicest person I had met since being taken away from my mother. I adapted quickly as I had always done and made friends immediately with the other residents.

I was enrolled at nearby Northside High School to resume my tenth grade year. I would soon be reunited with some of the students that I met while attending Humes Junior High the previous year, which included Tamara, the girl who I had a crush on; she had befriended a girl named Daphne. The three of us bonded as friends while customarily meeting and talking regularly during lunch period. We also took Economics together.

Back at the group home, I learned how to shoot pool and became really good. I played it all of the time and was totally addicted to the game. There was also a basketball goal in the backyard which I shot a lot of as well.

The group home was on the corner lot, with the backyard being enclosed with a chain-link fence. There was an old detached garage without doors; that is where hung out when outside. The driveway leading from the garage was sloped and facing Dunlap.

The basketball goal was at the top of the driveway which made it kind of challenging because of the slope of the driveway. While trying to play basketball, we were seemingly always going uphill when driving towards the hoop.

The first person I befriended at Porter Leath was Tyrone. He had been there the longest and became my mentor. He was a seventeen year old, slim, dark-skinned, black guy and showed me a lot of things; he also had a million-dollar smile. I personally don't like my smile. If you notice in most of my pictures, I don't show my teeth. It's not because they are crooked, missing or yellow; they are actually straight and white, but for whatever reason, I have never liked my smile.

He had been there long enough to have his own room which was decked out. He had his own stereo system, soldering iron and other neat electronic equipment. He also burned incense all the time. Yeah, ole' Tyrone was Johnny Cool. He even had a girlfriend who lived down the street on Dunlap; her name was Mary. She was an eighteen year old, dark-skinned, pretty black girl.

A Father's Double Life

I had only been at Porter Leath for about two weeks, when in late January of 1982, Tyrone wanted to talk to me. He lit up a cigarette, took a deep drag and then began.

"Mike, I don't know how to say this man, but my girl likes you."

"Are you serious?" as I got excited, but then regained my composure.

"Are you serious?" I said again, but more calmly.

"Yeah Man. She's seen you a couple of times and likes you."

"I don't know what to say. I thought she was your girl."

After he took another drag, he said, *"Well she is, but I can't stop her from liking someone else."*

"What are you saying?"

"I'm saying if you want to talk to her, then you can."

"I don't know what to say. I feel really bad about this."

"Ah, we were having problems anyway, and besides, you red-bones get all the girls."

"Huh? What are you talking about?"

"You light-skinned guys; you guys get all of the girls; us dark-skinned types don't have a chance against you guys."

"That's not true. You are just as handsome as I am and you have a great smile."

"Yeah, but we're a dime a dozen in Memphis. You red cats are few and far between. So if Mary wants to talk to you and you are down with it, I don't mind."

"Are you sure?"

"Yeah man, everything is cool. The next time she comes over, I'll officially introduce you guys, Okay?"

"Okay."

That was a very awkward situation for me. I liked Tyrone as a friend and knew that he adored Mary. How could he pass her on to me so easily?

It was also after that very conversation when it suddenly occurred to me why I was always being picked on. I then thought about every guy who had bullied me. They were all dark-skinned with the exception of Stacy, but I was even lighter than him. It also explained why Robin wasn't picked on as much as me, well at least until he got to high school anyway. Would I have to be treated like a leper my whole life just because I was of light-complexion?

Other than me wondering why I had been picked on, I guess Tyrone had informed Mary that she was welcome to visit me, because the very next day, he introduced us.

The doorbell rang and Tyrone answered with me in close proximity. We then stepped onto the porch where she was waiting.

"Mary, this is Michael. Michael this is my ex-girlfriend, Mary."

"Hello Mary, how are you doing?" I said.

"I'm fine, Michael," she said, while blushing and smiling from ear to ear.

Tyrone just shook his head and went back into the house as the screen door slammed shut.

"Would you like to go to the backyard? I asked.

"Yeah, that's fine."

After getting to the backyard, I was kind of speechless. I didn't really know how to carry on a conversation with a girl, so didn't know what to say. So I said the first thing that came to my mind.

"You got some really big titties."

She looked down at them and then back up at me with a big smile, leaned forward and kissed me on the lips.

"Gee, I must have said the right thing." I thought to myself

I saw fireworks for the very first time; her lips were so soft and felt like cotton. She pulled away and looked into my eyes.

"And you have some really beautiful eyes, Michael."

"I do?"

"Yes, what color are they?"

"Light brown."

"Uh-uh." I said, while she moved in closer to get a better look.

"They are light brown, but they have a green tinge around the outer edges. They are gorgeous."

"Thank you." I must have turned beet red.

I leaned forward for another kiss and for the next ten to fifteen minutes, that was all we did, just kiss. I then asked if she wanted to go shoot some pool inside which is exactly what we did, after she said, *"Yes."*

After getting into the house and walking into the recreation room, Tyrone was already shooting.

"Do you want to shoot a game of pool?" I asked. *"Naah – you guys can have it. I'm done."*

"Are you sure?"

"Yep, I'm cool; I'm going upstairs."

"Okay."

I must say that Tyrone was quite the gentleman throughout a very awkward situation.

After he left the room, Mary and I shot pool; she actually wasn't that bad. We played for about an hour and she then left. She would come over to visit me every day after school and every day, we hung out in the detached garage and just kissed.

We kissed all of the time and grinded against each other, but that was the extent of our little excursions. All I knew how to do was kiss, which turned me on. I never tried to take it any further and that was how our little visits went; we just kissed. I never tried to undress her, sleep with her, or even suck on her breasts. I just wanted to kiss.

I guess after about a month of all that kissing, Mary had had enough of my innocence and she and Tyrone were back together again, which was fine with me. But all of that kissing had me interested in girls, big time. My fear of intimacy was slowly fading.

I was definitely becoming more curious, but I also realized that if I was going to lose my virginity, it was going to take the girl to be the initiator and therefore the aggressor, because it wasn't going to be me.

Chapter 15
Blue Balls

I MET SUCH A GIRL AT Northside High in March of 1982; her name was Sheila. I was sixteen and my fear of girls was dissipating. I had already experienced, witnessed and gone through a lot in my very short life, but especially the last twelve months. I was quickly becoming a man.

NORTHSIDE HIGH

Sheila was very curvaceous and also very sweet. She approached one day in school and I initially shunned her, because she had a terrible case of acne, but she was absolutely crazy about me. She would pursue me, catch me in the hallway from time to time and steal a kiss from me. She again, was so nice and her body was bodacious, but it was her face that was almost hideous, but her personality eventually won me over. Before I knew it, we were soon talking and then walking home together after school.

One Day while walking home, guess what we did? Yeah—kiss. We tongued as you call it and were like animals when we kissed. She took me to her home and I knew that even though she wasn't the most attractive girl, she would certainly be my first because she just had that aggressive nature about her.

While over her house one day with her mother at work, we were watching the tube. Her home resembled the same kind of shack that I had lived in on Trigg, only it was white on the outside and not as nasty looking on the inside; actually very neatly kept.

Since living on Trigg, it had always been a habit of mine to look for roaches when entering someone else's house; I saw none in hers. If I ever walked into a home and saw a roach, I wouldn't eat or drink anything from that household and if I sat down, I would always sit on the edge of the seat, just so I would be well aware of any roach that might be crawling near me and therefore, be able to move away with a quickness.

I thought that roaches were the most disgusting, filthiest and nastiest things on earth. I'm sorry, but when you have had bad dreams of the creatures and then awakened in the middle of the night with them crawling all over you, well, it was definitely a phobia that I developed from living in that situation while on Trigg and I still have to this day. Trust me, I wasn't trying to be Bougie.

After not seeing any creepy crawlies, I felt comfortable enough to lie on the couch. Sheila pulled my pants down below my butt cheeks, while sitting on the floor next to me. I looked back and she had a pen about to write on me.

"What are you doing?" I asked.

"I'm doing something, just be still."

So I let her have her way.

After she finished writing on my ass, she got me a mirror so that I could see her artwork. She had drawn a double layer cake on my butt and below it, wrote *"Beef Cake."* She explained it to me and we laughed together while I pulled my pants back up. I know fellows, stupid thing to do, right?

It was after I pulled my pants up when I actually got the courage to ask her,

"Do you want to have sex?" I just wanted to get the mystery over with.

"I am a virgin Michael."

"So am I, I think."

"What do you mean, you think?"

While thinking to myself, I was actually unsure whether I was a virgin or not, because of what my father had done.

"Michael, what do you mean, you think? You are either a virgin or not. Have you ever had sex?"

"No."

"Well then, you are a virgin."

"Oh, okay."

"Anyway, I'm not having sex until I get married." She said.

"Okay, well that's fine with me."

Of course, I found out later in life that you don't ask a girl if they want to have sex, you just go for it when the situation presents itself. So instead of pulling my pants back up, I should have pulled them the rest of the way down and just gone for it, but I was totally oblivious when it came to girls, and besides, I didn't know how to have sex anyway. What would I have done once my pants were down?

I guess you could call Sheila my first official girlfriend because we walked home together, ate lunch together and spent a lot of time at her house.

During the school day, other kids, both boys and girls, picked on me because Sheila was ugly with all of her Acne and to top it off, she also wore very provocative clothes. It was because of her overall appearance that everyone had the impression and relayed to me, that she was a slut, a whore, nasty, and called her every other name in the book, because of how she looked, but I was un-phased. I was spending a lot of time with her, so I knew better and didn't let the negative comments deter our relationship.

She was actually becoming very beautiful to me. Her personality, charm, inner beauty and good heartedness made her very beautiful and for that matter, I saw nothing but beauty when I looked at her. I didn't see the acne or any other ugliness; I saw 100% beauty.

Sheila and I decided to take the scenic route home one day after school.

Well actually, if you had ever been in North Memphis around that time, there was nothing scenic about it. Most of the buildings were run down, the houses dilapidated and most of it just ghetto. You could always tell when you were walking or driving through the ghetto because there was always a pair of old tennis shoes hanging by the shoelaces over a telephone line.

North Memphis was also, where a lot of crimes and murders were committed and still is to this day, if you watch The First 48, like I do.

But in the midst of all of the ugliness in that part of the city, we found a beautiful grassy field and lied in it. Shortly thereafter, we were rolling over each other, just kissing and kissing. She would softly bite my lip and I would do the same to her. She then did something that would give me the erection of a lifetime; she put her lips on my neck. Oh my gosh!! She sucked on it for a minute and stopped, but I quickly directed her lips towards the same spot.

"Suck harder baby." I said.

With her big, soft, luscious, wet, sensuous lips on my neck, I melted like butter. I didn't know what sex felt like, but I couldn't imagine it feeling better than what I was experiencing at that very moment. She pulled away from me.

"Can you do the other side too?" I asked.

As she started sucking the other side of my neck, I didn't want her to stop. I was in total and complete ecstasy.

"Suck it harder baby. Oooo... Ahh…, oh my gosh, that feels so good baby; keep it going."

I was turning into a freak.

I then reciprocated by sucking her neck as we continued to roll in the grass. After about thirty minutes, we finally got up and started walking again; I had a major hard-on.

We weren't walking for more than ten minutes when I felt this excruciating pain in my testicles and penis. The pain was so bad that I could hardly walk and the agony only got worse. Sheila thought it was funny and laughed constantly while I moaned and whined in agony.

My dick wouldn't go down for anything. You would have thought I had swallowed a whole bottle of Viagra which of course hadn't been invented yet. Yep, she had laid a number on me without doing anything more than sucking on my neck and kissing me.

As we continued walking to her house, my pants were bulging. I kept tugging at my meat while trying to get it to go down. She was laughing at me, but at the same time was trying to console me as she put her arms around me and kissed me.

"Is my baby going to be okay?"

"Oh, I'm hurting so bad. What's wrong with my dick? It won't go down."

"Sounds like you got a case of the Blue Balls."

"Blue Balls? What's that?"

I pulled my pants away from my stomach and took a peek while using my other hand to pull my ball-sack up and to the side.

"My balls aren't blue."

"Not literally crazy. It's just the term for a painful and erect penis?"

"Oh.... Okay."

I then started wondering if she was actually a virgin or not. How did she know so much and how could she have done this to me without having sex? If this was the kind of pain that making love caused, then I wanted no part of it. Screw that.

We finally got to her house and said our good-byes as I headed home. It was on that particular day that I learned the art of masturbation.

I made it back to the group home, went upstairs, straight to my room and closed the door. I then put my birthday suit on, lied on the bed and started playing with myself. The next thing I knew, I was stroking it. I started slowly and then sped up. I must have been stroking it about three hundred times a minute. In a very short time, I was feeling great while moaning and groaning. Suddenly while screaming out loudly, I released the biggest scream and the largest load of semen I would ever see released from my penis in my life. Yes I was looking at it.

The load must have shot three feet in the air and all over me, actually getting some on my face. Hey, hey, it was my sperm okay. I looked down again and it covered my chest, my stomach, my thighs, my sheets and just about anything else within a three-foot radius.

Hazel must have heard the screams, because shortly after my outbursts, she opened my bedroom door, while concurrently asking,

"Are you okay Michael?" while I was still holding my semi-erect shaft in my hand.

I was so embarrassed and I guess she was too, but she stood in the doorway and stared at me for a couple of seconds with her mouth wide open. She eventually closed the door while I was still gasping for breath when I finally replied.

"I'm okay."

Yes, on that day, I had learned the art of masturbation. I learned it so well over the days, months and years to come, that I would put the MASTER in the word, because I did it regularly, at least five times a week, if not every day during some stretches. I had found a new toy; MYSELF. Of course, my father had done it to me a couple years prior, but I personally had never tried to sexually gratify myself until that day.

I got up, went to the bathroom and took shower, but only after looking in the mirror. My neck had passion marks all over it. They were a dark cherry red and covered both sides. I actually thought they were pretty cool and smiled about them. After admiring my hickeys, I went ahead and took my shower. My dick and balls were feeling a lot better—and relieved.

After getting out of the shower, I got dressed and went downstairs for dinner. Dinner was nice at Porter Leath. We all sat at a real dining room table and ate like civilized people. We said grace and passed the food around to serve ourselves as I thought to myself,

"Now this is what life should be like. I have a girlfriend, I live in a nice house, I have my own room, I have freedom and I am being a kid."

While daydreaming to myself,

"Michael, what's that on your neck?" Hazel said.

"Somebody got some booty," Tyrone then chimed in and passed a food dish to me.

I began to blush, but didn't say anything and wasn't about to contradict what he said, but little did they know, I was still a virgin.

"Man, she is a cannibal," David said; he was new to the group home.

"She tore that neck up. What's her name, Hoover?" Hazel said.

"Her name is Sheila." I replied.

"No, with suction like that, her name is Hoover, like the vacuum cleaner."

Everyone at the table laughed as I continued to blush something awful.

"Don't worry Mike, at least you got some booty," said David.

I just shook my head, while the subject finally changed, thank God. Little did they know, I hadn't had my cherry popped, but didn't say anything. However, if I thought I was being teased about my hickeys on that night, just wait until the following morning.

I went to school the next day while trying to wear a collared shirt that would somehow conceal the marks on my neck, but they were so deep, so red and stretched across my neck something fierce that there was no hiding them.

While walking down the hallways, to and from my classes, and especially at lunch, over the next several days, until they faded away, I heard the following comments from various people no matter what their gender.

"Man, she got you."
"You slept with that slut?"
"She's a prostitute."
"You better get tested for gonorrhea."
"Another one bites the dust."
"Dude, your neck is fuuuccckked up."
"So tell me Michael, was she a good lay?"
"You slept with that ho?"

Maybe I should have defended her and therefore myself, but I never did. I just listened and kept on my merry way. I didn't know why everyone had that perception of her. I guess the fact that she was ugly and wore tight clothes that didn't necessarily fit her right, gave everyone a bad impression of Sheila. Not to mention, her hair wasn't that well kept either, usually looking nappy and undone.

A lot about her appearance had to do with her being poor. It was just her and her mother and her mom was doing the best that she could to support them; I understood that.

Miraculously, through all of the unkind words, I didn't let them sway me from wanting to be with her and we continued to see each other. I guess for me, it was kind of neat having someone as crazy about me as she was, no matter what others thought.

Back at the group home, I was getting better and better at shooting pool as nobody, hardly ever beat me. Hazel had become like a second mother to me and was as sweet as could be. She liked listening to Teddy Pendergrass and was crazy about him. She was therefore devastated when he was involved in an accident in the Rolls Royce he was driving. It struck a tree in March of 1982, which left the legendary singer paralyzed from the waist down. Hazel was also very easy to talk to and she cared so much about us. She was a beautiful person and I will never, ever forget her.

Aside from my love and affection for Hazel, but in a motherly type way, I still had more things to experience. Remember how I was introduced to marijuana at The Runaway House? Well, I was introduced to alcohol at Porter Leath.

Michael Cavicante

We were playing basketball in the backyard one mid-spring night in 1982. There was Tyrone, David, and myself; oh yeah, and Tyrone's girlfriend Mary, who was watching us play.

Tyrone sent one of his friends who just happened to live directly behind us on Dunlap, to the store for some Malt Duck. To this very day, I still don't know what it is. I am not a big drinker, but we had some that night.

His friend came back with a thirty-two ounce bottle of the stuff and Tyrone went into the house, got some glasses, came back outside, poured us some and we all drank. I must say it wasn't long afterwards that I was unable to hit the backside of a barn with the basketball, because I was buzzing pretty darn well. Tyrone sent his friend to get some more, and again, we drunketh of the cup.

I don't know if you could classify us as drunk, but we were acting pretty foolish. Tyrone was throwing the ball off of the backboard so hard that I thought it was going to break; I was tackling David when he went for lay-ups and David was also trying to kick the ball into the hoop, rather than shoot it. Okay, okay, I guess we were pretty wasted. The night ended with Mary going home and us making it to our beds, crashing out for the night.

I woke up the next morning feeling pretty awful and I had a terrible headache. I also felt sick to my stomach which is what I found out to be a hangover. I didn't know why anybody would ever want to get drunk on purpose and feel that way, but I somehow managed to make it through the day.

Not long after that incident, my tenth grade year was over and so was the relationship with Sheila. Through all of the crude comments, I actually reveled in the attention that she gave me. It was probably something that I needed in my life at the time. I will never forget her and the *"Blue Balls"* she gave me as we said our goodbyes.

With Sheila in my rear-view mirror, the summer was upon me. Without a court hearing, I got the news that I would soon be going home. I missed my family, but I was finally living the life at Porter Leath and actually had mixed feelings about the possibility of having to leave.

Though I loved my mother dearly and knew that absolutely no one could ever replace her, I loved Hazel as well and now looked to her as a mother and the residents as my siblings.

I had been there long enough to have my own room with a door, I didn't freeze while trying to sleep in the winter and I didn't sweat while just

A Father's Double Life

sitting around the house on summer days. I didn't have to walk through urine-smelled rooms and most importantly, I didn't have to worry about whether my father was ever going to touch me again. For the first time in my life, I was happy and living normally. I didn't want to give it up, but knew that I had to.

I sadly said good-bye to the tenants of the group home as well as Hazel. It was a sad day for me, but like I had always done, I sucked it up and moved on.

After getting home, I saw my little sister Wendy for the first time in over a year, which brought a big smile to my face. It did feel good to have the family back together, but I didn't understand why the lights were off.

Chapter 16

Lights Out

It was a sweltering, hot summer day in 1982 with temperatures approaching a hundred degrees, when Robin, Wendy and myself, were back home on West Ball Road. My mother was happy and so was my father. Yeah, she stayed with him. My mother was from the old school, which meant, when you marry, you marry for life, regardless of the hard times, financial difficulties, and yes, even incest and child molestation.

Even though my father was job-hopping, one thing that I couldn't take away from him was that he had always been a hustler and therefore was able to provide some support and stability at times.

He greeted my siblings and me by giving us all a hug. I myself was especially happy to see my little sister. She was twelve years old and had grown up a lot in the last fourteen months since being removed from our home. I hugged and kissed her and told her how much I loved her. She still hadn't a clue as to why we were taken away from our parents, nor did she ever ask.

She was the apple of my father's eye and he was her idol. Even after everything we went through, I myself, amazingly, still looked up to him. Yes, there was some hatred as my childhood was completely stripped away from me, but I had to try and get over it, move on and not let it hold me prisoner for the rest of my life, so with that being said, let's get back to reality.

Even though it was daytime, I noticed that there wasn't a light on in the house. I walked over to turn on the television and it didn't power up.

Michael Cavicante

"*Why won't the Television come on?*" I asked.

"*The lights got cut off honey. We couldn't afford to pay the light bill.*"

"*Are you serious?*"

"*Yes baby, but we will get them turned back on.*"

In an instant, I was already wishing that I were back at Porter Leath.

In Memphis at the time and still maybe to this very day, you had one utility company, and its name was—MLG&W (Memphis, Light, Gas & Water).

That's right, one utility company controlled all of the utilities, so—if you didn't pay your whole bill, not just one, but all of your utilities were cut off. I always thought that was kind of messed up. You couldn't pick and choose which one you wanted to pay because it was considered one bill, so if you couldn't pay it, MLG&W turned off all the utilities.

With that being said, not just our lights were cut off, but our water and gas as well, so we couldn't bathe, cook, or watch television.

My father was still driving a cab and my mother wasn't working at all. I guess driving a cab wasn't cutting the mustard, but he explained to me how it worked.

A dispatcher called him to let him know where a pick-up was. If he was in the vicinity, he made the pick-up and then turned the meter on. Whatever it read when the customer was dropped off is what the customer paid, but before he could keep a dime, the first thirty-five dollars each day went to the company and on top of that, he still had to pay for gas, so it was kind of a hustle as well.

As the days passed, we all talked about our stays at the different group homes and got re-acquainted. Life for the most part was back to normal with the exception of course, the power being turned off.

The house was already not insulated, so the fact that there was no air conditioning made it terrible; you might as well have been living outside. At least outdoors there was an occasional breeze.

We had great neighbors on each side of us, Doris to the right and Tina to the left. Doris was a middle-aged black lady who was married and had three precious daughters. Their names were Lillian, Nadiera and the eldest was Ain. Our neighbors were significant, because we would fill up our bathtub with water by running a hose from Doris' outside water spigot. We then used that water sparingly for various reasons.

To bathe, we dipped a bucket into the tub to fill it. We then poured half the bucket into the sink and used a bar of soap and washcloth to bathe while standing at the sink, with a towel placed under our feet to limit the amount of water we got on the floor. After washing, we drained the sink, put the stopper in and then poured the other half of the bucket into the sink to rinse. That was how we kept ourselves clean.

To flush the commode, we simply filled the bucket up with water and then poured it into the toilet bowl until it purged. Go ahead and try it the next time your water gets cut off. Just kidding, I hope it never happens to you, but as a toilet works on gravity with the water coming from the tank, it pushes the waste down the pipes which is why the reservoir is placed higher than the bowl.

To eat, well let's just say that we ate a lot of sandwiches. Food, what little we had, was kept in Tina's refrigerator while other items needed for immediate use, such as milk and juice, were kept in an ice cooler. By the way, the tub of water lasted about three days, before we had to refill. Tina was an older white lady who lived with her husband Larry.

Within a few days after returning home, I was reunited and playing basketball again with Willie, along with hanging out with the other neighborhood kids. Willie and I hugged each other as if we hadn't seen each other in years. However, it was very embarrassing when Willie came over to my house to visit one day.

"Let's watch some TV Mike."
"Uh… its quiet time in the house right now man."
"Oh… okay."

I hated lying to my best friend, but I was so embarrassed, I just couldn't be honest.

While outside playing and it became dusk, my other friends would ask me,

"Why is your house so dark?"
"Uh…. well, my parents go to bed really early."

I think everyone eventually figured it out though; they just didn't say anything.

I had to do something to help out, so I went and found another summer job through C.E.T.A. I worked at Overton Park while riding around in a truck during the day for the Memphis Park Commission; I was a passenger.

Our job was to keep the park clean by emptying trash, cutting grass, working in the rose garden and other tasks. Minimum wage had increased to three dollars, thirty-five cents an hour which wasn't a lot, but when added to my father's income and after several weeks, it was enough to help get the lights turned back on. I was happy to be able to contribute.

During that summer, my father was trying to make amends for all that he had done wrong. He got out in the front yard and played catch with me while throwing the football. He also took me out and treated me to ice cream at times, but with the money I had given him from my earnings; I didn't say anything though.

My mother had wrecked the 1976 Thunderbird on the front side and though the fender was replaced, it was a different color from the rest of the car which was red; the fender was painted brown. We just couldn't seem to keep a nice looking car around and that was my father's biggest complaint.

Being a great truck driver and also receiving a safe driving award with Gordon's, my father never had an accident, but I guess my mother wrecked enough cars for the both of them. She was a good driver, but had slow reflexes. Does that make any sense? Okay, maybe not.

He really tried hard to make up for what he had done, but I had forgiven him long before because that is what my mother had taught me to do. He still had evil ways and even though he never touched me again, he said mean things to my mother which was just like abusing me, because it hurt me also.

He called her names in front of us, as my mother was a big woman described in the beginning of this story. My father was short, but had developed a gut as big as a whale and was tipping the scales himself at over two hundred pounds, so he had some nerve.

When they argued, he called her fat ass all of the time and told her,

"Why don't you lose some fricken weight?"

That was the word he used, "fricken." I guess he used that in place of the other "F" word. That's right, with all of his faults, I never really heard him swear, except for maybe dammit or shit. Needless to say, my mother's self-esteem was ruined. There were times when I heard her say under her breath,

"Go to hell." after he bashed her.

One time when she said it, he must have heard her, because he got up and raised his hand at her as if he was going to hit her, but didn't. I never saw him hit my mother, but the verbal abuse she took was probably just as bad.

At times I felt like a coward for not standing up to him, but he had us afraid of him because he got so angry at times; I guess it was that hot

A Father's Double Life

Italian blood. My mother told me that he once pulled a gun on her while living on Trigg, but I don't recall it, so it's not in this story.

My mother started going to Church by herself regularly and I attended with her sometimes. We attended Christ Missionary Baptist on South Parkway; there's that street again. Periodically, we got there in time for Sunday school as Robin and Wendy also attended. I always enjoyed reading out loud during Sunday school. I loved reading out loud.

After Sunday school, we went and sat in the sanctuary at around ten forty-five. I always loved the first Sunday because at eleven o'clock sharp, the organ would be played, the drummer was drumming and the Adult Choir marched in while singing. It was quite a treat.

I always got into it while clapping my hands and moving my lips as if I knew the words to the song being sung. The choir wore blue, satin like robes and swayed from side to side while marching in lockstep towards the front of the church. As there were two aisles, there were also two separate lines, but the chorus would converge and ultimately took their positions while facing the congregation behind the pulpit.

It was always a glorious event and boy could they sing; they had that church rocking. I would clap my hands and stomp my feat to the beat of the music and so would my mother. It seemed as if church was her only escape from the torment of my father.

My only complaint was that we were required to stand, even after the choir stopped singing and took their seats. We seemingly stood forever some more while listening to others speak and make announcements. We probably could have sat down, but out of respect and because everyone else was standing, we also stood. After about thirty to forty minutes of standing, we were allowed to be seated, but only after the Reverend took the podium and said,

"You may now be seated."

I didn't always want to attend worship services though. One Sunday, my mother asked me if I was going to Church with her. I told her that I didn't want to go and went back upstairs. The little boy who used to beg to go to church was getting rebellious. My father then came upstairs,

"Go to Church with your mother."
"Are you going with us?"
"No, I'm not." he replied.

It was at this point when I finally lashed out at my father. As my eyes filled with tears, I yelled at him.

"How dare you tell me to go to Church when I have never seen

you step foot in a Church you hypocrite! How dare you tell me to go to Church after what you put this family through! How dare you tell me to do anything! How dare you try to be a father now! You stay away from me and stop calling mom names, you bastard, you dirty, filthy bastard!"

All the hurt, all the pain, all the anger, all of the sadness and all of the frustration had suddenly come out. I was crying pathetically while sliding down the wall into a crouched position and nestled in the corner of my room. I then looked up and watched my father while he sat on the edge of my bed and started crying himself with his face in his hands.

For the first time in my life, I saw my father cry and for the first time in my life, I had disrespected him. I just watched while he sat on the edge of that bed and cried like a baby.

I felt bad about what I had said and wanted to go over and console him, but something wouldn't allow me to do so. I just sat there and watched. I sat and cried again as I wrote this part of the story, more so than I have cried with any other part I have written, for a son should never have to say these awful things to a father, but on that day in my life, it had to be done.

After several minutes, he got up and left without saying another word while I stayed in my room for the remainder of the day. It was after that episode, that I think my father finally started to respect me. It took some work, but over the next three years we eventually became closer and talked more.

Chapter 17

Pac Man Fever

I KNOW YOU HAVEN'T HEARD A lot about my sister Wendy as of yet, mainly because she was almost four years behind me and really was never a problem. However, she was twelve years old, light-skinned, pretty, thin and very funny. At times, she would out of the blue, prance into the living room and make the funniest faces I had ever seen and then retreat back to her bedroom which is exactly what she did in this early 1980's photo catching her at her zaniest.

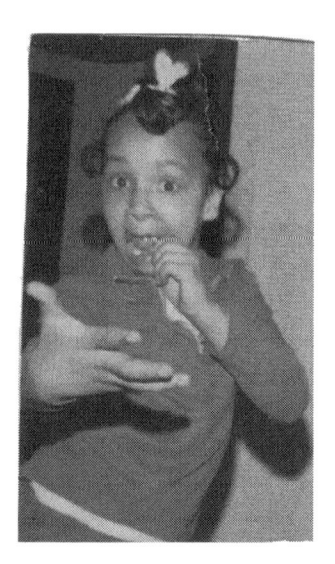

MY SISTER WENDY

Michael Cavicante

Wendy also became used to having her way and was never disciplined by my father. There were times when I would ask my dad for a dollar for whatever reason and he would say,

"I'm broke."

Wendy would come right behind me and ask for a dollar, and he would say,

"Go get one out of my pants pocket."

This happened many times as I thought to myself and in astonishment. Now that I think about it, maybe she went and asked him for a dollar right after I did, just so I could witness him giving in to her as if to throw it in my face.

Wendy also never got a beating from him and was never scolded or yelled at. I was the only one that gave her any discipline. I think it was for that reason she looked up to and respected me because we hardly ever fought. She and Robin on the other hand, were always into it. She always antagonized him and they would fight (verbally) quite often.

As mentioned earlier, when Robin got angry, he bit his right wrist and grabbed his crotch with his left hand while stomping his feet. He would then stomp upstairs and we could always hear him when he plopped on the bed.

As Robin got older, we started to realize that even though he was mentally slow, he had a lot of smarts and not just common sense. I guess we always realized it, because the things that he said and did often surprised us.

Robin also had a fascination with electronics because he regularly took apart radios and tape recorders just so he could see how they operated. For those particular actions, he got yelled at a lot, because he was very destructive in that manner. The electronics never did get put back together. That went on for years as he upset my parents constantly.

He was also bed-wetter as I mentioned earlier. He wet the bed often and wouldn't say anything about it. There were times when he actually lied atop the urine soaked mattress, even after awakening. My father beat him at times and eventually he stopped, but until he did, his room smelled awful and at times was unbearable. My mother also had to make him take baths. He was seemingly afraid of water.

On a positive note, Robin did introduce me to Ms Pac Man. There was a new Ms Pac Man video game at that same gas station where I was sent to pick up items for the family. At the age of sixteen, I had never played a video game before, but I played one time and was hooked.

A Father's Double Life

I started by clearing the first two boards, then the first five, the first nine, then thirteen. I would get in a total zone and couldn't be caught by those four ghosts. I made it so far—that eating the energizers wouldn't make the ghosts change colors. They would just go in the reverse direction. I was totally addicted.

The owner of the gas station, Gerald, usually gave us free games to play and because of that, I was there every day. I guess he knew we were poor, and—he liked us as well. It was common for him to open up the machine and click twenty or thirty free games on it. Robin and I played endlessly. It was our new form of entertainment when I wasn't at work.

I got so good that Robin would never beat me as he did have a knack for being very good at video games. Ms Pac Man to this day is my favorite video game. My high score is 754,000 points and one of my personal Email addresses is even dedicated to it, mspacman754k@aol.com , so e-mail me when you finish reading my book and let me know what you thought of it.

Please type **I Read Your Book** in the **SUBJECT area of the Email**, so that I may be able to separate and identify these particular emails, or they may certainly go unanswered. I will try to respond to as many as I can. Or go to my FAN PAGE on FACEBOOK and JOIN the FAN PAGE of *"A Father's Double Life,"* as well as leave comments. In the meantime, let's get back to the story.

That was also the summer when I made the personal decision to stop taking my Epilepsy medication which was still Dilantin. I was determined that I wasn't going to be held prisoner by that disease. My mother told me that I needed to take it so I wouldn't have the seizures. I told her that I wouldn't have any more seizures and from that point on, I stopped taking the drugs.

My mother consulted with a doctor and he told her that kids do sometimes grow out of Epilepsy, however it was not known when it happens, because they usually continue taking their meds and the meds are usually considered the reason as to why they aren't having seizures.

When not playing Ms Pac Man, I was busy working at the park while my father also hustled to make money. I watched him go to pawn shops with regularity. If he could get a buck for it, then it was going to be pawned.

His new thing to earn money was going to the blood bank. Every eight weeks, he went and gave a pint of blood in exchange for ten dollars. In a nutshell, he did have some good qualities. He never just sat around the house and was always trying to find a way to put food on the table and clothes on our back; he wasn't a lazy man. While my dad was hustling, Willie was working full time hours at The Commercial Appeal which was the local newspaper, so we weren't spending as much time together as normal.

He worked on the fifth floor, and no, it wasn't a psychiatric ward. However, from some of the people that worked up there, it should have probably been one. How do I know? You will find out soon. Willie's brother also worked there. You see, their father had been a long time employee and had some clout, so he was able to get both of his sons employed there as well as their sister, pretty eyed Jackie.

While Willie was working steady, the summer ended and so did my job. I had saved out a few bucks to buy some clothes to start the school year with, but would be repeating my tenth grade year at yet another school, Southside High, in September of 1982.

SOUTHSIDE HIGH

I think it was obvious why I had failed the previous semester. I had spent eight weeks of the school year in Juvenile Hall, but somehow, someway, managed to pass tenth grade English; don't ask me how. I just know that I was taking eleventh grade English while still a sophomore.

I actually wanted to go back to Oakhaven, because Coach David had said that I would be his starting tight end, but I guess the school zoning laws had changed and I was forced to go to Southside. The only thing I liked about going to the school was that Willie, my best friend, was going there, but he was a senior. I still had three more years to go. However, Southside was mainly a predominantly black school and very popular, so I was a little excited about attending.

I did go out for the football team that year, but had my heart set on playing tight-end or fullback, but the coach wanted me to play on the offense and defensive line, because of my size, standing six-feet and weighing in at two-hundred thirty pounds. I declined to play, quit the team and tried to concentrate on school.

Meanwhile, back at home, my dad was trying to be a better father, but his mistreatment of my mother was heartbreaking. The verbal abuse continued and I started to wish that she would leave him, even if it meant being homeless, but she was committed to us and didn't want us raised in a broken home. She was strong for staying with him while enduring the years of abuse and ultimately became my hero. Speaking of heroes, my dad, being born in San Francisco, was a 49er Fan.

The 1982 NFL Season was about to start and he was excited about his team. They were coming fresh off of a Super Bowl win over Cincinnati, 26-21 in January of that year and their future looked bright. Their starting quarterback was a big reason for that and his name was Joe Montana, who was my dad's new hero.

On Sundays, my father wanted me to watch football with him. I did reluctantly, but only because I was trying to form some kind of bond between us. He sat on the couch and watched 49ers games when they were on television which was seemingly every week at the time. The football team was good and seemingly always won and he carried on like a fool.

Other than Sundays when I watched football with him, most of my time if not at school was spent outside in the neighborhood playing sports with Willie and the other neighborhood kids. I went home as late as possible; sometimes as late as eight or nine on school nights just so I wouldn't have to look at my father and continue to witness the relentless bashing of my mother.

She could very well write her own life story about what she went through with him and the pain she endured. If I knew all the intricacies of what she actually dealt with, I would write if for her. I am sure that she has kept more from me than I am actually aware of.

While attending Southside, I had always taken pride in the fact that even though my grades weren't the best, I had never failed a grade. However, it seemed like my life and future at the time was uncertain, so I guess having to repeat my sophomore year didn't hurt anything. I buckled down immediately and for the first time in High School, I made the Honor Roll. I was ecstatic.

I went home and showed off my report card. My mother was so proud of me. I then went and showed my dad who was sitting on the couch. I wanted him so badly to be proud of me too.

"Dad, I made the Honor Roll." I said as I handed him my report card.

"Why don't you go clean your nails, they look awful."

"Okay dad."

"Here, take your report card."

I must say that all the wind was taken right out of my sail. He rarely had anything good to say and that particular day was no different. I was generally extremely clean and of very good hygiene; probably the most hygiene conscientious person in the house, next to him of course. I brushed and flossed three times a day and took baths and showers daily while always ensuring that my fingernails were well trimmed and clean, but he would have to say something negative. It was just his nature to bring me down.

I had my next crush in my eleventh grade English class. She was a thin, light-skinned, petite female and sat near the front of the class. I think she liked me too, because I caught her looking at me every day, but throughout the whole year, I never said more than two words to her. I could tell that she had class and was from a well-to-do family, so maybe I also thought that she wouldn't have anything to do with me once she found out about my family situation, even if I was brave enough to approach her.

I guess another problem that I had was that I felt inferior to the girls that I liked. I had pretty good taste, but just figured they were too good for me. I however regretted for a long time that I never said anything to her. She was so sweet, quiet, very smart, and always dressed nicely while wearing penny loafers, cardigan sweaters and designer jeans. Yeah, she had it going on, but I never had the pleasure of getting to know her.

Chapter 18

Determined to Work

As the school year continued, the money struggles in our family continued and seemed almost non-existent; money that was. We could never go anywhere or do anything. It seemed as if we were condemned to the house, the neighborhood and therefore the city of Memphis.

I had a taste of working from the summer before and wanted to work on a regular basis. It gave me a sense of self-worth and pride to be able to help my family. I started wondering if Willie could hook me up with a job at The Commercial Appeal, so I talked to him. After our conversation, he told me that he would see what he could do.

Willie was a great friend. He often gave me money to buy snacks whenever we went to the store. He also brought food from his own household in order to help my family survive. If he wasn't doing that, he was inviting me over for dinner. He made me feel at home while at his house.

I would always raid the cookie jar and he would have to tell me to only get two or three, because if he didn't, I would grab ten. I told you my mother never taught us portion control, and besides, I loved cookies. His mother, as well as Jackie, always welcomed me with open arms, treated me like one of their own and always asked if I needed anything.

As far as hooking me up with a job, Willie came through. He told me to be down at the loading dock in back of the building which was on Beale Street, at seven-thirty, Saturday evening; I was to ask for Bill. Needless to say, I was overcome with joy and could hardly wait.

Well, Saturday night arrived in mid-November, 1982 and it was pouring down rain. I didn't know where my dad was, but he knew what time I had to be there, so I waited patiently for him. The clock struck seven o'clock, then seven-fifteen and then seven-thirty.

"Where is dad at?" I asked with anxiety.

"I don't know," my mother replied.

Even though the time had already come and gone as to when I should have been down there, I had to somehow show up—and by any means necessary.

After brainstorming as to what on earth I should do, I threw on a windbreaker, went outside, jumped on a bicycle that had a flat tire and in a torrential rainstorm, pedaled seven miles to The Commercial Appeal. I traveled the interstate because that was the quickest and most direct way to get there.

I hadn't traveled more than a block when I was about to make the decision to go back home, but making a u-turn wasn't an option. I pedaled up Rutgers, because I figured the descent of the first hill, would carry me up the second one, but when you have a flat tire, the momentum I had hoped for was non-existent. I then had to pedal up the second hill, which was steeper than the first, but made it nonetheless, then crossed the fork in the road and was soon out of the neighborhood. I made a right turn onto Norris Road, crossed the bridge that goes over the interstate, crossed the street, and then four lanes of traffic onto the interstate.

While taking the acceleration lane onto I-240N, there was nothing about that bike that was picking up speed. Cars sped past me while honking, even though I was clearly on the shoulder of the road, but I wasn't going to be deterred.

The front tire was coming off of the rim and even though I could hear the metal hitting the hard pavement, I wasn't about to give up. I must have been either crazy or desperate, maybe a little bit of both.

I heard the traffic approaching from behind and thought that maybe it was better if I was facing the oncoming traffic while on the other side of the freeway so I could see the automobiles before me. However, it was too late for all of that non-sense; I had to keep going.

As pelts of rain battered my face, my mission was unstoppable. While wobbling, I heard the loud horn of an eighteen-wheeler approaching from the rear.

"What is that trucker's problem?" I thought to myself.

I turned my head only to see the big diesel approaching at startling speed, which in turn scared the crap out of me. I then looked forward and hit an object, only to fall off the bike and into the grass while the trucker sounded his whistle on the way by. Thank God I fell to the right and not to the left which would have landed me onto the road and into the truck's path. I wouldn't have lived to tell this story.

While sitting on the ground, I was about to go into a mental breakdown and started crying, but after about five minutes, I regained my composure, mounted the bike and continued my trip. After traveling another three miles or so, I finally exited Union Avenue West while cycling over the flyover that doubled back over the interstate. I saw traffic light after traffic light, seemingly going through at least ten, before arriving at The Commercial Appeal. I was almost there.

While still raining heavily, I got off of my bike, walked it across Union and then another block over to Beale Street. I then jumped back on the bike and rode another block to arrive at the loading dock in the back of the building at around eight-fifteen, but there wasn't a soul to be found.

I laid my bike down on the sidewalk. I don't think I had to worry about anyone stealing it. I then went into the Security Guard Station located just outside of the loading dock where there must have been at least a dozen monitors with a sentinel watching them.

I walked up to his post as he stood to greet me.

"May I please see Bill?" I asked.

"Why do you need to see Bill?"

"He was supposed to hire me tonight."

The rent-a-cop looked over at the monitor that viewed the loading dock.

"The loading dock is empty. He's already hired everybody he needs for the night."

"Well, can I go upstairs and see him?"

"Not without a guest pass. Do you know anyone in the mailroom?"

"My friend Willie works up there."

"Is he working tonight?"

"I don't think so."

"Listen kid, I'm sorry, but I can't let you go up there."

"Can you call the mailroom and ask if Bill can come downstairs?"

I think to appease me, he called upstairs while I stood there in anticipation that something good was about to happen, but after he got off the phone, he told me,

"Bill is busy and even if he weren't, it isn't customary for him to come downstairs to meet someone; okay? Now you need to leave kid."

Michael Cavicante

"*Okay.*" I replied, while hanging my head and turning around to exit the building.

I was about to get on my bike and head back home, but I had made the trip and therefore made the decision that I wasn't about to leave until I got what I went there for. There had to be another way.

I went outside, peered at the loading dock and figured that there had to be a different route to the mailroom. The wharf was empty, but a big door was open. I walked closer, then up the stairs and onto the platform. I peaked inside that big door and saw what looked like an elevator. I looked around, didn't see anybody and jumped on it. It was a big, freight type lift, the size of a room; it was easily eight feet by eight feet.

I pushed the close button when a door from the bottom and from the top started to come together as I thought they would meet. I then let go of the button and they opened back up. I tried it again and as the doors closed, I let go of the button and they opened back up again. I started to panic and wondered what was wrong with that stupid contraption. I then saw a man walking slowly towards me from about fifty feet away.

THIS IS THE COMMERCIAL APPEAL LOADING DOCK WHERE
I WAS SUPPOSED TO BE AT SEVEN-THIRTY AND THEN
EVENTUALLY SNUCK ONTO THE ELEVATOR. IT IS WHERE
WE WAITED TO BE HIRED ON VARIOUS NIGHTS.

"Hey, what the hell are you doing?"

It was at that point that it dawned on me that I had to keep the button depressed for the doors to close completely. While holding my finger on the button, the guy starting to run towards me, and as he was getting near, the doors finally closed completely. I hit the number five button and was on my way up to the mailroom; whew, close call.

The elevator got to the fifth floor and I had to keep the open button depressed also. They didn't open automatically either. I exited the elevator and just stood there. Still soaked and wet from the rain, I watched in amazement while a lot of people, both women and men worked tirelessly. What a busy looking place I thought to myself when a guy approached me. Looking as if he could have been seventy, I thought he was too old to be working in such a busy place; his name was Rudy.

"Can I help you young man?"

"I'm looking for Bill."

"It looks like you got caught out in the rain young man."

"Yes sir."

"Anyway, Bill is sitting right over there." As he pointed him out to me.

"Thank you, sir."

"You can get some hot chocolate in the canteen over yonder."

"Okay; thank you sir."

"You're welcome son."

As I slowly approached Bill, he was busy directing others on what to do while planted firmly on his stool. He was a middle-aged white man and very distinguished looking. His hair was neatly combed and styled off to the right. He also had a mustache and beard. He was smoking a cigarette when I arrived within speaking distance.

"Are you Bill?"

"That's me. Who are you?" he said, after exhaling his second-hand smoke.

"My name is Michael Cavicante. I know I was supposed to be on the loading dock at 7:30, but my ride didn't show up. Willie had told me to ask for you."

"Your ride didn't show up? That's probably not a good thing to say." he replied.

"I know it doesn't sound good, but if you allow me to work, I will never be late again sir, I promise."

"Listen—what's your name again?"

"Michael, Sir."

"Listen Michael, I'm sorry, but I've already hired everybody that I needed for the night. Why don't you try back next week, okay?"

As huge crocodile tears started to fill my eyes, I replied,

"Sir, I need you to please hire me. My family needs money, winter is coming and I don't want our lights to be turned off again. Please hire me, sir. Please."

Bill looked at me for a second, got up, walked me to an office and then had me fill out an employment card. Afterwards, he took me to insert machine number four, showed me what to do and walked away.

"Thank you sir for hiring me; thank you very much," I said, with a big smile on my face.

"You're welcome Michael," he replied as he looked back.

I would hand-up to Karen for the remainder of the shift and didn't mind at all. She was a doll baby. A brown-skinned, black girl in her early twenties, she was attending Memphis State University. We talked all night long. I told her my story of how I rode my bike in the rain and got hired; she was totally amazed. She was the first person I met at The Commercial Appeal, other than Bill, and oh yeah, the cocky security guard.

I had jeans on and they were soaked. I could have definitely used Richard's clothes dryer and had wished it were there in the mailroom. Needless to say, I was miserable, and handing-up was backbreaking work, but I was young, strong and running off of pure adrenaline, so I was up to the task. I would hand up until four thirty in the morning with the exception of a meal break at eleven-thirty.

To explain to you what handing-up is; the main body of the newspaper came off of the printing press from four floors below. They were sent up to the mailroom via wire conveyor, went into a stacking machine and then released, at which point, they were stacked on a push cart by human bodies and then taken to the insert machine.

At the insert machine, the main body of the paper was placed on a feeder, which dumped it into a bucket. The bucket then circled the machine and other sales inserts from department stores were dumped into the main body, via identical feeders. Those inserts were delivered to the paper company already pre-printed on large skids which is what those huge freight elevators were used for.

On each insert machine, you had a feeder and a person handing up. That was the person giving the feeder the stack of inserts to put on the machine which is what I did. After they are put onto the machine, something resembling suction cups grabbed them and they were dumped into the main body of the paper as it went around in a circle and eventually exited the machine, via another wire conveyor, that took the completed newspaper to another machine which stacked the newspapers.

The stack then exits and goes down a roller conveyor while another person placed a wrapper on the stack of newspapers. The stack was then compressed and tied by another machine and afterwards slid down a five-story chute to the delivery trucks that are loaded. The newspapers were then taken and dropped off at designated locations for their carriers to pick them up for delivery; and that my friend is how a newspaper was put together.

I must have handed-up a thousand times that night as I did every night I worked for a while. I don't even remember who took me home that morning, but I arrived home at five o'clock, knocked on the door and my mother let me in. I told her about my long night while she told me how proud of me she was. I then took a shower and went to bed.

The job worked on seniority, so the longer you worked there, the more hours you got every week. How it worked was, based on the amount of inserts they would be using on any given night also depended on how many people they needed, so Bill knew every Saturday night how many people he needed minimum, for the following week.

He would make his rounds around one a.m. on Sundays to sign people up for the following week. If you weren't at work on Saturday night, he called you at home. We were called casuals because we weren't with the union and therefore considered part–time, even though we could still work full time hours.

Of course, it would be awhile before Bill ever came by and saw me on a Saturday night for any extra shifts to give me, but at least I was guaranteed one shift a week which was cool. However, if I wanted to work more hours, then all I had to do was be down at the loading dock on other nights.

The busiest nights, aside from Saturday, were Tuesday, Wednesday and Thursday nights. If one of the full-time time employees called in, or if the night was going to require more manpower than originally projected, then Bill would need extra people to work and there I was on the loading dock while ready, willing and able while showing up on those nights.

Sometimes I got picked up to work, sometimes I didn't. My mother waited for me in the car until she knew for sure. My father still didn't trust my driving enough to allow me to take the car to work on my own for such a distance. If I got hired, she would leave and pick me up later. That's if Willie wasn't working, otherwise, he would take me home when I got off.

Chapter 19
Not Again

It was December and Christmas was upon us. The temperatures are dropping below freezing, there was hardly any food in the home and as every winter would have it while living in that house, it was very cold.

There was a fireplace in the living room, but instead of burning wood because we couldn't afford it, we roasted our trash to help keep the house warm. We used mainly plastics, because they cauterized longer, but would stink up the house with an awful smell. We lived in a wooded area, so we were able to find kindling to help keep the fire going.

My father was filling up the bathtub and sinks with water. As my intuition would have it and without my parents saying a word, the lights, gas and water were about to be cut off again, and sure enough, the next day, they were; darn that MLG&W. Yes, I was working, but the two or three nights I was getting a week wasn't enough to help keep the lights on, which was my sole reason for wanting to be employed.

It was bad enough for the lights to be cut off during the summer months, but now we had to endure the winter, and even worse, Christmas without electricity. At least during the summer months when we washed up, the water was bearable, if not at times refreshing, thanks to the heat, but to wash up in a cold house with cold water was absolutely miserable.

I shivered and shook while I stood there in front of the sink naked trying to bathe myself. While in bed and trying to keep warm at night, I curled like a baby in a mother's belly while trying to sleep.

The only good thing about the lights going out in the winter was that we could sit milk and juices out on the back porch to keep cold, which is what my father did. After I prepared a bowl of cereal in the mornings, my mother went out on the back porch, retrieved the milk and poured it over my corn flakes. I must say that the milk was nice and cold, but so was I.

Candles were used to light the house at night, just like they were during the summer when we lost our electricity. My dad had the nerve to get mad and was going off, because he was missing his 49ers on television; yeah, he was a stone cold trip. I wanted to tell him myself, that if he could keep a job or make more money, then maybe the lights wouldn't have been turned off, but I wasn't about to make him feel worse than he probably already did.

As the month of December continued while Christmas came and went, we were still out of school for the holidays. During those couple of weeks, I went out during the day and looked for wood to burn in the fireplace. Times not spent looking for wood, were spent at Willie's nice and warm home. I spent a lot of time there during the day.

Willie's brother, Chris, was big on music and loved Michael Jackson; shucks, who didn't love Michael? The big difference between Chris and I was that he could afford to buy all of the latest albums, and at the time, there was no record bigger than "Thriller".

I just so happened to be visiting Willie, when Chris came home, pulled it out of a bag, opened it up, pulled the vinyl disc out, blew it off, just to add a little showmanship and then placed it on the turntable. As the first song played, Chris began into his groove and put on a show for us while dancing to *"Wanna Be Startin' Something"*. I thought Chris was so cool and at times, hilarious.

While sitting there, I observed the surroundings of the warm home. Jackie would walk through the room and joked Chris while he was dancing to the music. He then gave her a love tap on the back of the head as she walked by. She gave him an evil look with those big ole pretty eyes of hers, but kept on walking. Willie was beating on the table to the rhythm of the music and their mother was serving cookies and milk. It was quite a nice atmosphere.

As the Michael Jackson hits continued to play, I pondered to myself,

"Now this is how a real family is supposed to be; fun-loving, happy and carefree."

For the first time in my life, there was some jealousy.

"Why did I have to be born into such a defunct lifestyle?"

After spending several hours at Willie's, I moped back down the hill and to my dysfunctional family. There was no doubt in my mind that I loved them, but just wished conditions could have been better.

Conditions would soon improve and after almost a month without electricity, our lights were turned back on just before the end of the year. There is a saying that is very true.

"You never really appreciate what you have until it's gone." Ain't that the truth?

With the holidays over, it was 1983, school had started again and it was too cold to walk, so my mother took Robin and me to school in the T-Bird; you know, the two-tone automobile which was also falling apart. I was in high school now, you know the time when you are trying to fit in with the rest of the kids. It didn't help to be dropped off in front of the school in a car that looked like this.

Have you ever seen the movie *"UNCLE BUCK"*? John Candy is dropping off his niece and seemingly a hundred kids are around watching when she is about to get out of the car and it backfires? Tia, I think her name is in the movie, looks at him and asks,

"Has anyone ever embarrassed you this badly?"

John Candy looks at her, while thinking for a second and then says,

"No." As she just shakes her head and gets out of the car, after they make the agreement as to when she will be picked up.

Yeah, that is probably how I felt when my mother dropped us off. Of course, I never told her I was embarrassed, but when I got out of the car, I held my head down and almost ran out of the automobile in order to limit the amount of people who saw me.

There were females galore at Southside and I couldn't let them see me get out of such a hooptie, but outside of the cutie in my English Class, there was only one other girl that caught my eye; her name was Kim. She played basketball and was the only reason I went to the girl basketball games. She started for the team, along with her older sister.

I watched her as she ran up and down the court. I never thought a sweaty woman could look so sexy, but she did. She had the most gorgeous eyes and the perfect body. Man was she hot, but of course, I never approached her. Willie and I usually went to watch both the boys and girls play. He always paid my way.

Southside had a great male basketball player that year; his name was Ernest. I just happened to attend a game in which he made a great play. There were only four seconds before halftime and the other team was about to inbound the ball. Earnest pretended to be going back down court to defend, but just as the other team inbounded the ball, he quickly doubled back, stole the in-bound pass, dribbled once and swished a three-pointer as time expired. The crowd went absolutely ballistic as I then thought to myself,

"*I bet he has a lot of girlfriends.*"

I think it was obvious that I was girl crazy, but without a clue as to how to attract them. I was just too introverted. There is no way you would believe that if you saw me today, but back then, I pretty much kept to myself. I was very humble and soft-spoken. I guess a bunch of humbling experiences would make anyone that way.

I thought that maybe a good way to find a girl was to take a Valentine's Day picture; that's what I thought anyway. They were being taken at school and I thought that being in the presence of other high school girls while getting their pictures taken would be a good way to get some attention; I was wrong.

HERE I AM TWO WEEKS BEFORE MY
SEVENTEENTH BIRTHDAY; FEBRUARY, 1983

All of them were with their boyfriends. I was the only idiot to take one alone and it wasn't even a good picture of me. If I looked tired, it probably had something to do with the hours that I was working. As a matter of fact, my work schedule in conjunction with my home life probably had everything to do with how I looked.

A few days after my Valentine's Day Mug Shot, my seventeenth birthday was quickly approaching and I was anxious to get my driver's license. Seventeen was the age at which you were able to apply. I don't know why I was so hell bent on getting a license actually, because we didn't have a nice car to drive, but when you are a teenager, you just want to drive, regardless of how embarrassing the family car may look.

I was able to coax my dad to take me to the DMV and get a Driver's Handbook so that I could study for the written exam. Surprisingly enough, he also took me out several times to give me some pointers.

After about ten days of studying and on February twenty-eighth, my mother took me back to the DMV to take the test. I was so excited that I didn't know what to do. When it was all said and done, I had passed the eye and written exam, but failed the driving test.

Of course I was disappointed, but found out that I could go back and take it the very next day, which is what I did and then passed. I was absolutely ecstatic and now legal. My father was reluctant, but allowed me to drive periodically anyway.

Outside of driving occasionally, I was being introduced to our new neighbors. They included Wanda and Vanessa; both were really smoking!! Maybe since I couldn't land a girl at school, I could possibly have one of these cuties.

Wanda was light-skinned, sweet, curvaceous, pretty, and looked like a Barbie Doll. Vanessa had all of the same attributes, but was the dark-skinned version of Wanda.

All the guys in the neighborhood had a crush on Wanda. She had personality, a beautiful smile and was bangin' all the way around. However, she would belong to Stacy. Do you remember him? He was the guy who chased me with the skateboard and I subsequently beat up, but by that time, he and I were cool. Wanda was crazy about him.

I watched how giddy and happy she was when she was in his presence. I must admit, there was some envy there. I only wished a girl that beautiful would be as crazy about me. Even though my mother often told me how handsome I was, I never really believed it. I figured that she just told me that because she was my mother. I knew that I wasn't ugly, but otherwise,

Michael Cavicante

I was oblivious to my looks. I know girls liked me, and yes I was given compliments, but I never really let them go to my head.

WANDA THE TEENAGE HEARTTHROB

Stacy wore the IZOD (alligator) shirts that were popular back then, designer jeans and penny loafers. He always looked good and I was therefore no competition, while wearing faded no name jeans, no name shirts and cheap, no-name shoes.

The other girl, Vanessa, probably could have been just as liked as Wanda, but she stayed in the house most of the time and was rarely seen. I think her parents were very protective of her, but when she did show her face, it was always a pleasant experience.

There was also Lawrence. He was the dark-skinned version of Stacy, and like Stacy, he wore designer clothes and was always cracking jokes with me being the butt of most of them.

Lawrence and Stacy both dated Wanda, or at least that was the gossip

A Father's Double Life

in the neighborhood. Word had it though that Wanda only pretended to date Lawrence just to make Stacy jealous. Stacy was her heart. Well, enough of all of that.

Then there was the forgotten one who lived on Alcy; her name was Leslie. She was of light complexion, very cute and mature beyond her years, both physically and mentally, but like Vanessa, we rarely if ever saw her. We had all of these cute girls in the neighborhood and I couldn't land any of them.

While I was wishing for a girlfriend, it was the spring of 1983 and I had impressed Bill enough with my hard work and reliability, when while working on a Saturday night, he stopped by to see me.

"What nights do you want Michael?"

"Are you serious?"

"Yeah buddy, you've earned it; now, what nights you want?"

"Every night you got!" while smiling from ear to ear.

"Okay, you got Tuesday, Wednesday and Thursday nights, and also, Saturday's day shift."

"Really?"

"Yeah, you asked for every night I had." And he walked away, after penciling me in.

I was ecstatic and had a grin on my face as big as a Cheshire cat, but thought to myself,

"How am I ever going to work those hours and still attend school?"

Needless to say, the one time I made the Honor Roll, would be my last. Every night consisted of hours from eight p.m. to five a.m., but I was up to the challenge and worked thirty-two to forty hours a week while attending high school.

Sometimes in order to get my hours in, I worked Friday night from eight until five in the morning. I stayed at work, slept in the canteen area, woke up and worked again from eight until four in the afternoon. I then went home, took a shower, ate dinner and was back at work Saturday night, and worked from eight until five in the morning. Yep, I would pull twenty-four hours in a thirty-three hour time period, but I can tell you that I slept all day Sunday, sometimes not waking up until six in the afternoon.

Since I was working a lot and pulling late night hours, my dad eventually let me start driving to work, which was really cool.

I worked my way up from handing up, all the way to being an actual feeder as the years went by. I knew how to do everything in the mailroom practically. Yep, I had mastered all positions, from handing-up, to stacker, to loader, to feeder. I was a now a versatile employee and consistently got the hours I needed to help support the family. Each Wednesday was payday and I gladly handed over practically my whole check.

While continuing to work however, I wondered how I was ever going to make it through high school. I do know that I was extremely bright and was also blessed with a photographic memory that helped me a lot, because I never did develop good study habits, if I studied at all. I wanted to be able to study and make good grades and realized how important they were if I wanted to go to college, but was unable to because of work.

At that point, with the hours that I was pulling trying to help support my family, the question of the day would be,

"Would I even graduate?"

I guess that question would be answered later, but for now, I had finally passed the tenth grade.

Chapter 20
Loophole

In the summer of 1983, I was working steadily and wanted a car of my own. Do you remember Gerald, the guy at the gas station who gave us all those free games of Ms Pac Man? Well, he had a 1976 Pontiac Grandville for sale. It was similar to the Bonneville my father used to have.

He wanted five hundred dollars cash for it, but because he knew me, he put me on a payment plan and sold me the car. I was so excited that I drove it home and showed it off to my family. Everyone was happy for me except my dad; he didn't say too much. The car was brown and had beige vinyl seats. Yeah, vinyl covering was the interior of most cars back then, either that or velour.

The air conditioner didn't work and if you have ever driven a car in the summer with vinyl seats, it wasn't a pleasant experience as the seats got extremely hot. The seats became so hot, that if I had on shorts upon entry of the car, my legs would literally get scorched.

While dealing with the hot vinyl seats, I was driving all over Memphis when one day while cruising down Third Street towards the downtown area, I saw what looked like steam coming from underneath the hood, but kept the pedal to the metal anyway. I looked down at the gauges and saw a red light flashing, but kept motoring along. It seemed as if my car was slowing and puttering even though I had my foot planted firmly on the accelerator. I heard horns honking and saw cars zooming pass me while some people even gave me the finger.

It eventually became apparent to me that something was definitely wrong, so I pulled over into the next available gas station. While frustrated, I slammed the car into park and then pulled the hood release and got out. I then heard what sounded like boiling water while trying to lift the hood, but the steam being released was so hot that I couldn't grab it with my bare hands. A gas station attendant then came over with a towel wrapped around his hand and pulled the hood up for me. After lifting the hood, a big cloud of steam escaped and blew right through my face. There was also green stuff sputtering all over the engine.

"What's wrong with my car?"

"It's just running hot. You probably need a thermostat."

"Oh, okay, but in a car?"

"You know what a thermostat in a house is, don't you?"

"Well, yeah."

"Okay—a thermostat in the car does the same thing; but it controls the temperature of the engine."

"Okay."

"You just need to let it cool down and then put some more water and anti-freeze in there."

"How long will it take to cool down?"

"About thirty minutes."

"Okay."

I then went and sat on a nearby curb and waited for the car to cool off. I had about twenty bucks on me, so I went into the station and bought some anti-freeze. The attendant came back over and helped me while also adding some water. I was soon back on the road and driving; that's before the whole situation repeated itself less than forty five minutes later while on Mallory Avenue and only minutes from home. After pulling over to the side of the road, I left that car sitting right there and walked to the gas station where I purchased the automobile. After a sweltering twenty-five minute walk, I arrived at the store.

"Why are you walking?" Gerald asked

"Because the car you sold me doesn't work."

"Where is it?"

"I left it parked on the side of the road, over on Mallory. It ran hot on me twice today."

"Well I'm sorry to hear that Michael."

"Yeah me too; can you take your car back?"

"What? You don't want it?"

"Nah, I don't think so. I didn't know that the a/c didn't work and those seats get awfully hot. Besides, I can't afford to pay for the gas."

"Well, I'm sorry it didn't work out for you Michael. I'll send a tow truck to go pick it up. Where is it at, on Mallory?"
"Yes sir."
"Okay Michael. Do you want to play some Ms. Pac Man?
"I don't have any money."
"I'll put some games up there for ya."
"Nah, I'm okay, but thanks anyway."
"No problem Michael."
"Thanks for giving me a chance to buy it, I really appreciate it."
"You're welcome Michael."

Sweaty, frustrated, tired and disappointed, I left the gas station while hanging my head. I hadn't even had the car two weeks and it was nothing but trouble; I was walking again. After finally getting back home, I walked in the house and was greeted by my mother.

"What's wrong honey? Where's your car?"
"I had to give it back."
"Why?"
"Too many problems and besides, I couldn't afford to put gas in it anyway?"
"Awe, well I'm sorry to hear that." she replied.

My dad was sitting on the couch watching television when the peanut gallery spoke.

"I guess you thought it would be all fun and games. Now you know that owning a car is a big expense and isn't a toy. You got to learn the hard way."

I didn't even respond. I just grabbed a clean change of clothes, took a shower and went to my room for the rest of the evening while saddened over the loss of my ride.

On the upside, something else happened that summer. I wore shorts to work for the very first time and low and behold how the women stared. I had never experienced anything like it. Remember—this was 1983, which was a time when men wore shorts that exposed their thighs. I was whistled at like crazy and had even more women approaching me just to talk. I was totally amazed. My legs didn't necessarily turn on high school girls, but older women were certainly aroused by them. From that day on, I wore shorts all of the time.

I enjoyed the attention so much that I even wore them in the winter months. Yeah, I finally realized that my mother did know what she was talking about in reference to my muscular legs and milk bottle calves.

As the summer came to an end, I was trying to find a way to get back to Oakhaven for my junior year because I remembered what I had been told by Coach David about being the starting Tight-End in football several years prior. I had a passion for football and wanted to play a skilled position. I was gifted with exceptional hands and could catch any pass thrown to me, but wouldn't be given a chance at Southside.

As evident by how I got hired at The Commercial Appeal, I was at the point in my life when I started going after whatever I wanted and I wanted nothing more than to go back to Oakhaven, so I discovered a loophole that would get me back there. All I had to do was find an academic class that Oakhaven offered and Southside didn't. After doing some research, those classes were Etymology (the study of words and their origins) and Greek Mythology.

It was time for the '83-'84 school year. After the second time around, I had made it through my sophomore year and was about to start life as a junior at Oakhaven. I would therefore be bussed again which I didn't mind. It meant that I would never have to walk to or from school, or have to worry about being dropped off in the old jalopy of a car we owned.

I was also working steadily and able to stay dressed nicely. Just before school started, I was able to purchase my very first pair of Nike shoes which was the highlight of my shopping day. I tried them on and walked around in them while in the store. It felt so good to see the famous swoosh on my kicks; it was like a dream come true. I couldn't believe that I was actually wearing a pair of Nikes'. I also bought a couple of pairs of Levis and some nice shirts.

I went out for football and made the team. However, my heart was set on playing tight end or fullback, but I was in for a big surprise. A new coach had taken over and his name was Woody. I think a woody is what he had for me because he never gave me a chance to play anything but tackle. He explained to me that we had a small team and he needed my size on the line for blocking. Well, I wasn't argumentative as a kid and accepted his reasoning which didn't mean I necessarily agreed with him or that I liked it, but I accepted it nonetheless.

The biggest guys on the team where, Willie, Kenneth, Terrence, Terrance and myself and we would all played both sides of the ball while on offense and defense. Yes, there were two Terrences and both were our all-district linebackers on defense. We ran a 5-2, which meant five guys on the line of scrimmage and two linebackers. I reluctantly played and was a starter, but wasn't happy.

ME ON FOOTBALL GAME DAY IN THE FALL OF 1983

I had been smart enough to figure out how to get back to Oakhaven, but wasn't smart enough to make a phone call, only to find out that David was no longer the Head Football Coach; what a bummer. I knew that I was a special talent because not only could I catch anything thrown to me, I was also a load to bring down when carrying the football. On top of that, I could also throw the ball sixty yards or so and in a tight spiral, but then again, so could Jamarcus Russell, so maybe that isn't saying a whole lot. I tried to show off in practice during warm-ups while hoping the coach would take notice, but he never did.

Both Terrence and Terrance often criticized me, because they knew I had the potential to be a great lineman, so they wanted me to get any notion of playing running-back/tight-end out of my head. But still, during pre-practice warm-ups, I ran routes and allowed guys to throw the ball to me just so Woody could see me while hoping to make an impression upon him.

If I were as aggressive back then as I am now, I would've gotten a chance, because I would have confronted him verbally, but never did. Woody might have been his name, but a Woody Hayes he wasn't, because a good coach would have noticed my skills just as Coach David did, but it wasn't to be and our football team was less than impressive and lost with regularity. The football season ended and life went on.

Looking for some other extra-curricular activities, I signed up for the Math Club because it was my favorite subject and thanks to Richard teaching me how to play Chess, I joined that faction as well.

Christmas came and went as usual as we moved into 1984. It was February and my eighteenth birthday arrived. After school, I got home, went into the house and Willie greeted me at the door. There was a cake and balloons as my mother was standing at the table. They had thrown me a surprise birthday party; it was Willie's idea. They wished me happy birthday and Willie told me that he loved me. I hugged him and told him the same as he gave me my first birthday party in a long time. It was one of few nice memories while I continued working long hours and going to school.

I was so tired from working and continued to sleep on the school bus as well as in class. No one had a clue as to what I was going through except for Willie. It wasn't something I volunteered unless asked.

School nights were especially rough while arriving home between four and five in the morning. I would take a shower, catch a nap, only to be right back up at six o'clock, in order to catch the six forty-five bus to school. If the hours ran over, I wouldn't get home until five-thirty, in which case I didn't get any sleep at all. I just went home, took my shower, ironed my clothes, got dressed, ate breakfast and then trudged to the bus stop while half asleep.

I'd get on the bus, have a seat, lay my head against the window and slept all the way to school while other students played, laughed, talked and joked. At times, I'd have to be awakened when arriving at school as drool ran down the side of my cheek. I'd depart the bus, find a bathroom, throw some cold water on my face in order to somewhat revive myself and then find my way to Homeroom.

At the risk of being repetitious, this is how it went for me for the remainder of high school and almost every day. I was often scheduled to work on those busy Tuesday, Wednesday and Thursday nights, but if not lucky enough to be penciled in, I still went down and stood on the loading dock in hopes of being hired if someone called in sick. Again, Saturday nights were automatic and guaranteed me at the very minimum eight hours a week.

Was I ever going to see any light at the end of the tunnel? In Junior High, I was dealing with what my father had done and Mid-South Hospital. Through high school, I endured four foster homes while also attending four different schools in five years and on top of all that, I was working nights until five in the morning while pulling forty-hour workweeks. How could I have possibly made good grades? Somehow miraculously, I managed to pass the eleventh grade, but barely.

Chapter 21

Car Notes

It was the summer of 1984. My father and I were talking more while trying to have some type of relationship. It wasn't easy, but he tried to form a bond with me that had long been broken. I still loved him, but hated what he had done to me as well as the family. If I could have turned back the hands of times, I would have stopped him, stood my ground and maybe things would have been different, but it was too late for all of that. What was done was done and I had to start thinking about what to do with the rest of my life.

Thanks to dear old dad, I still had another year of school left, but what would I do after that? My grades weren't good enough to get a scholarship or a grant for that matter. My parents were broke and couldn't afford to send me to college and my football coaches never gave me a chance to play anything but tackle. Of course, I realized later in life that offensive and defensive linemen get scholarships too, so maybe, just maybe, if I had applied myself, who knows what could have happened. I wasn't oblivious to it, but just thought I would have a better chance of getting recruited by a college while playing a skilled position.

While trying to decide on what to do after high school, I decided that it was time for another automobile. Thanks to my father finally finding another trucking job with Glen McClendon, I was able to save a little money, so I walked a mile or so, to a car lot on Elvis Presley Boulevard.

D and D Auto Sales was a small independent dealer not far from my home and also in close proximity to the Surplus City Store where I had been arrested several years prior. I never set foot in that place ever again.

I saw the car that I wanted as soon as I stepped on the lot. It was a blue, two-door, 1976 Ford Elite coupe. It had a white landau top and inside were those hot, white vinyl seats; it was awesome! I went inside of what resembled a trailer home and talked to the lady who owned the place. She was a very pleasant, middle-aged, black lady.

"How may I help you young man?" as she greeted me.

"That is a beautiful car." I replied.

"Which one?"

"That blue Ford with the white top. How much is it?"

"It is fifteen-hundred dollars."

"Wow, fifteen hundred dollars? That's a lot of money," I said, as I hung my head.

"How much do you have?"

"I only have three-hundred ma'm."

"Well, I can put you on a payment plan."

"I'm familiar with that, how does your payment plan work ma'm?"

"You give me the three-hundred and you pay the rest in weekly installments."

"And I can take the car; right?"

"Yes, you can take the car with you."

"Are you serious? Let's do it."

"Do you have a job?"

"Sure do ma'm. I work at The Commercial Appeal in the Mailroom."

"Really? What do you do there?

"Whatever they need me to do ma'm," as she just smiled with delight.

"Well that's good. I need a copy of your driver's license, a paystub and your three- hundred dollars."

I just happened to have a paystub on me, along with my driver's license. I handed her those items along with the three hundred dollars. Shortly thereafter, she went over the payment agreement with me,

"Okay Michael, your payment of forty dollars will be due every Friday."

"Okay." I was excited as could be.

"You will make fifty-two payments, after which you will receive the title."

"Title? What's that?

"It is a document that shows you are the owner of the car."

"Oh, okay." I still didn't understand, but signed the agreement anyway.

"Okay young man, you're all done. Congratulations."

"Really? It's my car?"

"Yep, here are the keys."

I gave her a hug and waited while she had someone put plates on. Afterwards, I got in the car, looked around the inside, adjusted my seat, started the car, and drove away. I couldn't believe that buying a nice car was that darned easy.

I could hardly wait to get home to tell my family, but after arriving at my house, walking in the front door while jubilant, my excitement didn't last long.

"Hey everybody, I got a new car!"

"What are you talking about?" my father responded, while sitting in his usual spot on the couch.

"I just bought a new car dad."

As I stood at the door, Robin, Wendy and my mother were all excited, while rushing out to see it.

"So how did you pay for it?" My father asked while seeming less than impressed.

"I have been saving money."

"So you've been holding back on us, huh?"

"What are you talking about?

"How much is your car payment?"

"Forty dollars a week."

"Forty dollars a week? Your check is only one-hundred ten."

"I know."

"You couldn't afford the last one you bought, what makes you think you can afford this one?"

"Well, I am working a consistent forty hours a week now and I figured you were doing okay working for Glen McClendon trucking."

"What I make is none of your concern. We need every penny to make ends meet. Another car is the last thing we need."

"Yes sir."

"So you go and buy a car without thinking it through. All you have done is hurt the family, that's all you've done. I hope you're happy with it. Maybe when we don't have a house to live in, we can sleep in your car."

Afterwards, he resumed watching television with his head resting in the palm of his hand and elbow on the arm of the couch; nothing more was said. I felt really bad and thought that buying another car was a big mistake. Regardless of my thoughts, I went outside while the rest of my family admired my new ride.

"It's nice Michael. I like it better than Richard's car." Robin exalted.

Richard had actually been long gone. His family moved to Texas in years prior.

"I'm proud of you son and you did it all on your own," my mother said as she hugged me.

"I like your new car Michael." Wendy said.

"Do you think I should've bought the car mom? Dad is mad at me."

"Honey, after everything you've been through, you deserve it; don't mind him."

"Are you sure mom? The family needs my money to help pay the bills?"

"Michael, he is just selfish. We will be just fine with whatever you're able to give us."

"Can you take me for a ride Michael?" Robin asked.

"Sure my brother, get in the car." His excitement level was off the charts.

My mother and Wendy went back into the house while I backed out of the driveway. I then headed to the corner of Ball and Rutgers which was the corner that all the neighborhood kids hung out. I stopped and briefly said hello to everyone. After being complimented on my new whip by all, I drove off and around town with my brother.

Robin seemed more excited than I was. He played with the radio dial and just about everything that had a button attached. After about an hour of driving, I returned home and walked in the house with my father in the same position I left him. He didn't say a word to me and I didn't say a word to him as the evening faded away.

The next day, I headed up to Willie's house. He had recently bought a Bonneville. Pontiacs must have been popular at the time. Do you know what they say Pontiac means? P̲oor O̲ld N̲igga T̲hink I̲t's A̲ C̲adillac. I guess that must have been true back in the day because it seemed like every black person I knew had one. I knocked on his door and told him to come outside. After joining me in the driveway, he asked,

"Whose car, Mike?"

A Father's Double Life

"It's mine."
"For real? It's nice man."
"Thanks, Willie."
"Let's go wash our cars together."
"Okay." I replied.

Soon thereafter, I followed Willie to the car wash and we cleaned our vehicles. After that day, we took turns going places together. He would drive his car sometimes and I would drive mine others. As you can tell, we were like brothers that had become inseparable.

As far as my car was concerned, it did finally dawn on me that the cost of keeping up my car would in fact hinder me from helping my family with its living expenses, so I came up with an idea.

I had been at The Commercial Appeal for eighteen months and was very well liked, especially by Bill. I would use that to my advantage, along with a certain charm that I was starting to develop.

While at work one night, I approached Bill.
"Hello sir, how are you doing?"
"I'm doing fine Michael, how are you?"
"I'm doing okay. Have you been working out?"
"No. Why?"
"Your biceps are bulging and your chest looks like it's getting bigger."
"If my biceps are bulging, it's from doing twelve ounce curls."
"Twelve ounce curls? What's that?"
"Drinking a lot of beer." He just smiled and shook his head while I also laughed.
"Well what about your chest getting bigger?"
"That comes from smoking," he replied.
"How's that?"
"Smoking makes my lungs expand therefore making my chest appear bigger."

I just laughed. I had no idea that Bill had such a great sense of humor. But I also thought to myself that buttering him up wasn't getting me anywhere when he then said,
"So, what do you want Michael?"
"What makes you think I want anything?"
"I'm an old man and very wise. My biceps are bulging and my chest looks bigger; give me a break and what do you need Michael?"

"Well, I was wondering if you could hire my mother to work up here?"

"Your mother? There is nothing I would take more honor in doing. Tell her to be on the loading dock Saturday, seven-thirty sharp."

"Are you serious? For real?"

"Serious as a heart attack. You're a fine young man and I would love to meet the woman who raised you. Just tell her to be on the loading dock Saturday night."

"Okay! Thank you sir!"

"You're welcome Michael." As he lit up a cigarette, I pranced away.

Other than trying to butter Bill up, my favorite person to converse with while at work was a guy named Harold. He was from Chicago and a very mature, intelligent, black teenager. He also had a brother that worked up there, Steven. Harold and I were lucky enough to work on the same insert machine most of the time and the conversations were always pleasant. We often talked about what our future ambitions were. I always knew that he was going to be successful and at the time, his idea of success seemed like a certainty as we talked that very same night after I chatted with Bill.

"Mike, I don't know about you, but I'm going to win the Illinois State Lottery," said Harold.

"Really?"

"Yep, that's how I'm going to become rich. I'm going to win that joker."

"Wow, that's cool. You seem pretty sure of it."

"Mike; it's a done deal. It's my destiny to win the lottery."

"Well, when you win, just make sure to look out for me; okay?"

"No problem Michael."

He sounded so convincing that I believed that he was going to win it. I was rooting for him all the way. Our conversation would carry on throughout the night and after putting in another eight-hour shift, I went home and got some sleep. After awakening, I gave my mother the great news.

"Mom, Guess what?"

"What my precious son?"

"I got you a job."

"What are you talking about?" as she looked in astonishment.

"I talked to Bill last night and he wants you on the loading dock, Saturday night at seven-thirty."

"I can't do that kind of work honey."

A Father's Double Life

"Yes you can, mom, its not that hard. You can do it. At least give it a try."

"Okay, I will be down there."

"Cool. You're going to do just fine, mom."

The very following Saturday night, my mom showed up on the loading dock and was hired to work. She handed up just as I did my very first night. I would keep a close eye on her while she toiled. She was going on fifty years old, but worked her butt off. I felt badly, because I didn't think she would be able to handle it and thought to myself,

"What have I gotten my mother into?"

But my mother not only handled it, she performed exceptionally well while keeping up with the fast pace of the mailroom. I checked on her periodically to make sure she was okay. Her make-up would run as she sweated badly. I brought her water or diet soda from the canteen time to time as well as paper towels so that she could wipe the sweat from her brow. I actually wiped her forehead myself at times.

"Are you okay mom?"

"Yeah, I'm fine; Bill is very handsome."

"Yeah—I guess so."

"Is he married?"

"I don't think so, but he dates someone who works up here."

"She's a lucky gal."

"Mom, dad is handsome and look how he turned out."

"Hmmm…you got that right. Looks aren't everything, but I just said he was handsome son, that doesn't mean I want to sleep with him."

"I know mom."

Just as my mother and I was finishing up our conversation, Bill just so happened to walk over, with a cup of coffee in one hand and a cigarette in the other.

"How are you doing Mrs. Cavicante?"

"I'm doing fine sir."

"Please, call me Bill. Sir makes me feel so old." My mother laughed.

"Yeah, I know what you mean," while she continued to labor.

"You got a mighty fine son ma'm."

"Yeah, he is quite a young man." I listened to the exchange and beamed.

"He's been through a lot," she said.

"Well, we're glad to have him. Everyone up here thinks the world of him. He's a hard worker. You've got a good one here," Bill replied.

"Don't I know it. Thank you."
"Well, talk to you later." Bill responded
"Okay."
Bill then walked way as my mother subtly shook her head.
"What's wrong mom?"
"Darn that man is handsome. He's got that rugged look."
"Mom."
"Well he is." while she continued handing up.

After giving her a kiss on the cheek, I went back to my work station and thought about how much I loved her and what a great woman she was, I mean absolutely great. I would have died for her if I had to.

Over the course of only a few short months and just as I had done, my mother earned more hours by her hard work. We would soon have more money coming into the house.

I actually wondered how my mother picked up more hours so quickly, but later realized that as she thought Bill was handsome, maybe he too, thought she was beautiful and had total control over how much he could actually see her. She also was quite the charmer.

Chapter 22
Imaginary Sex

The summer of 1984 ended and it was time to start my senior year at Oakhaven. Yes, for the first time since third grade, I would be attending the same school for consecutive years. I finally had some stability in my life.

I was playing football again and therefore still playing on the line. Other than my disappointment in football, the good news was that I was driving to school in my new car. For the most part, life seemed better, but what other disappointments would await me on the horizon?

One day during football season, Terrence, Wendell and I went riding in my new car before the game. It was ritual for the team to rest in the locker room between the end of the school day and the start of the competitive event, which was usually seven thirty in the evening, on either a Thursday or Friday. One particular game day, we went out in my car and were headed back to the school and only minutes away.

We had just come from under a tunnel which was actually a runway belonging to Memphis International Airport that ran across Winchester. There was a traffic signal at the top of the hill when you came out of the underpass.

It was pouring down rain when the light changed from green to yellow and instead of slowing to stop; I kept going and hit a pick-up. It was in the intersection preparing to make a left turn. He must have thought I was going to stop which is why he proceeded into the turn. Well, I didn't stop and as he made the left turn, I collided with the truck and destroyed my car.

There was only a small dent in the side of his vehicle, but my whole front end was demolished. The police arrived, took statements and I was given a ticket for running a red light. I actually thought it was his fault because the light was still yellow when I entered the intersection, but I got the citation. Unable to be driven, my car was towed and we were taken back to school in time for the game.

Oh yeah, I never did get insurance, because I couldn't afford it, so I would never see my car again. It was back to riding the bus for me. I had given up on driving for the time being and figured it just wasn't meant to be.

As far as football season was concerned, it was only one or two games into the season, when my knee got busted up. Needless to say, I was out for the rest of the year. I wore a leg brace that extended from my upper thigh to the middle of my calf. I would wear the splint for six weeks.

As I was maturing, girls were becoming more attracted to me. After all, I was working and able to dress better. Or was it because they felt sorry for me after seeing me hobble around from class to class?

One girl in particular, Jacqueline, took an interest in me. She was a Flag Girl and would help me down the stairs while I struggled with that leg brace. She was really sweet and seemed really genuine, and of course, it was an honor to be seen with a Flag Girl, at least back in the day anyway, because they were all beautiful. I was often questioned about our relationship and honestly didn't know how to respond except that we were just friends. Maybe it was that fact along with my lack of girl prowess that she would only after only a couple of weeks leave me alone.

Maybe I could have paid her a thousand dollars to pretend to date me and just like Ronald Miller, in the movie, *"Can't Buy me Love",* I would have turned into the object of every girl's desire, but the movie hadn't came out yet, and even if it had, I might have gotten the idea, but didn't have a thousand dollars. I wasn't a nerd, but might as well have been.

Meanwhile, back in the neighborhood one day, Wanda and I were walking down the street talking. Yeah, the same Wanda every guy in the neighborhood was crazy about and the same girl who was crazy about Stacy. I must say that I felt honored that day to be alone in her presence.

It was just the two of us, as miraculously we seemed to be the only people outside that day and what a beautiful autumn day it was. I couldn't believe that I was alone with and in the presence of the most beautiful girl in the neighborhood, if not all of Memphis. Yes, she was that darn fine. After talking and walking for a block, she looked me in the eyes.

"Michael!"

"What?"

"Your eyes."

"What about them?"

"They're totally green!"

"Totally green?"

"Yes. One hundred percent."

"No they're not."

"Yes they are. They are so beautiful; Oh My Gosh!"

"Well thank you," but I still didn't believe her.

And as she gazed into them even more while getting closer, I thought she was going to kiss me on the lips, so I closed my eyes while awaiting her lips to touch mine. I kept wondering what was taking so long when she said,

"Michael, open your eyes."

When I opened my eyes, she was back at arms distance apart.

"So much for that," I pondered.

We continued walking and talking a little more and then parted ways. I thought she was kidding about my eyes, especially after getting home and looking in the mirror. They were still light brown as they had always been, but then I figured,

"I was outside when she said that."

So, I grabbed a handheld mirror, went outside into the front yard, glared into the sun and then back into the mirror and sure enough they were totally green.

"*Wow!! My eyes change color in the sunlight,*" I wondered in amazement.

Wanda and I got closer, but friends were all that we would ever be. Do you remember Vanessa? She was the dark-skinned version of Wanda. She started riding my school bus during my senior year, but was dating Ralph. They would sit on the back of the bus and he treated her so badly while cursing and hitting her. I just shook my head, but it seemed as if she liked the treatment because she allowed him to continue, day in and day out.

Vanessa came outside periodically and we talked. I asked her why she put up with the abuse, but she really didn't have an answer for me. She did realize that I was a nice guy and after a while, we kissed every now and then, but that was as far as it ever went. The bottom line was, I was too much of a gentleman and never forced the issue, so at that point in my life, at the tender age of eighteen, I was still a virgin. I guess it also became apparent to guys at school that I was a virgin when one day, a guy asked me,

"Hey Cavicante. A girl has three holes. Which one do you stick your dick in?"

I was confused because I had never seen a vagina up close or otherwise and didn't know it had three holes, so didn't know what to say, but wanted to give an answer.

"The one in the middle?" I replied.

"Uh… okay," he said, but laughed at the same time, along with his buddies.

I stood there while not knowing why they were laughing when he then said,

"Mike, once you get some, you will never be at a loss for words when it comes as to what to say to a woman. You will always know what to say."

I didn't know what he was talking about and how finally having sex would change my approach with women.

While I was still wondering about the three holes of a woman, another football season was over, the holidays were upon us and I had only six months to decide what to do with the rest of my life.

Meanwhile, I was busy working for the holidays and accumulating some overtime, which was pretty much a guaranty during that time of year. While at work one night, I met Pamela. She was about five-foot two, one hundred fifteen pounds, light-skinned and cute as pie. She was twenty-one or twenty-two years old and boy was I totally and completely smitten by her, probably more so than I had been with any other girl in my life at that point.

I found out that she just so happened to be the sister of another girl with whom I had attended school at Oakhaven. I only had to speak with Pam one time and I was in love. There was just something about her that was unique. She was so special that I pointed her out to my mother.

"Mom, I think I am in love."

"With who?"

"Pam; she is right over there."

"She's cute." My mother replied.

"Isn't she though? I'm definitely in love."

"Those are some strong words. When did you meet her?'

A Father's Double Life

"Fifteen minutes ago."
"And now you're in love?"
"Yep."
"It's called lust. Your hormones are just raging, that's all."
"What's the difference?"
"Lust is when you desire someone out of purely physical attraction."
"Well what's wrong with that?"
"Because it is the inner beauty that counts. Outer beauty over the years fades away, and then what is left?"
"Well, until it does, I will be happy just looking at her."
"But when it does, will you leave her?"
"No, I wouldn't leave her."
"How do you know if the outer beauty is what you're in love with?"
"I guess I wouldn't know."
"Exactly. Learn what a person has to offer on the inside. That is what counts son."
"You got a point mom, but she is fine."
"Then its lust. You're not in love."
"Mom, I'm in love." My eyes were all dreamy.
"Okay son, if you say so."

I then went back and talked with Pam some more. She was so sweet and as delicate as a flower. I was definitely in love. When I took my breaks, I would run to the canteen and get her snacks. I can say that I was totally gone. She was so intelligent and oh so very fine to me. We talked all of the time, but she thought I was too young for her.

I knew where she lived, because again, I knew her sister. I would leave teddy bears, flowers and cards on her front porch. I was certainly the hopeless romantic. I was willing to do anything for a chance to be with her, but it wasn't to be. She liked me, but wanted no part of romance.

Life is so funny, isn't it? The person you want to be with never wants you and the person who wants to be with you—you never want. I guess that's just the way life is.

I wanted Pam so badly that I cried in my room one night when my mother came upstairs to check on me.

"What's wrong with you?"
"I'm in love with Pam, but she doesn't want me."
"Well she is the fool. Is that all that's wrong with you?"

"Yes."
"That's no reason to cry."
"But mom, I love her."
"Well, you can't make someone love you back son."
"What's wrong with me? Why don't I have a girlfriend?"
"Because you're different?"
"What are you talking about? How am I different?"
"You are a gentleman, you are kind, you are beautiful; women don't want that."
"What do you mean?"
"Women like bad boys, especially young girls. They aren't going to appreciate a guy like you and the kind of girl that would appreciate you is like trying to find a needle in a haystack."

My father then came upstairs and as I continued to talk about the things that I had done for Pamela, he asked,
"Is she a black girl?"
"Yes." I replied.
"Ain't no nigger woman going to appreciate that type of treatment. You need to be with a white woman."
"What are you talking about dad? I'm black."
"Yeah, but you got white blood running through your veins; and besides you don't look like a nigger."
"Then why did you hide me and Robin in the backseat of the car when we were younger?"
"It was mainly because of Robin, not because of you."

As my father turned to leave the room, my mother just looked at him and shook her head.

At the time, I never really knew or understood the racial heritage of my mother, but I never thought anything of the comment, because to me, she was my mother. I didn't really see color, even though she looked, talked and acted white, she was my mother. I guess I never exactly knew what to make of her at that age. I personally didn't care about color. Pam could have been white, black, Asian, Chinese, etc.; I didn't care. I just wanted a girlfriend.

While still crying, my mother told me,
"Michael you are a beautiful person. Look at what you have been through son and you are still a good person. You are caring, you are compassionate, you're a hard worker, you're handsome, and have a nice build on you. You are going to make some woman very happy."

A Father's Double Life

I then replied, *"I'm going to be mean and hit girls, because that's what they seem to like. They don't appreciate me. I'm just going to be hateful and ruthless."*

She grabbed my head with both hands and looked me square in the eyes,

"No you're not. You are going to remain the same good person that you are. Screw Pamela or any other woman that doesn't appreciate the way that you are. Look at yourself."

She then stood me in front of a mirror.

"Look at you. Shucks if I weren't your mother, I would go for you myself. You are an exceptional person and you don't have to change for nobody. You just continue being yourself and the right woman will eventually come along. Forget Pamela, if she doesn't want you, it's her loss. Do you understand me young man?"

I continued to cry, but responded,

"Yes mother. I understand." As I gave her a hug and she went back downstairs.

I masturbated regularly, but masturbated that night with thoughts of Pam on my mind. By this time, even though Robin's room was conjoined with mine, I had placed a sheet up at the dividing line in order to have some type of privacy.

I turned on some music, took off my clothes, pulled the blankets back and lie on my back. I then grabbed my penis and began stroking it while thoughts of Pam went through my head. My eyes were closed and I imagined kissing her precious lips while I continued to fondle myself. I hadn't a clue as to what being inside of a woman felt like, but I wanted my first experience to be with her.

As my dick became hard as a rock, I stroked it faster while softly calling out her name as if she were in the room with me, because that is where I wanted her to be. As the music played, I went faster and faster while pretending that she was with me.

I was in complete ecstasy when all of a sudden, that ecstasy became the start of an unleashing of tension, emotion, desire, passion and heat as I arrived at the ultimate of sexual healing. My body tensed up, my legs straightened and tightened, my toes spread as far apart as humanly possible, the grip around my penis got stronger and I released every ounce of that tension, emotion, desire, passion and heat, in the form of a semen eruption.

With little to no restraint, I screamed loudly and after a few seconds, my body relaxed as my legs loosened, toes contracted and the grip around my dick became non-existent. I just lied there breathless. I then knew that Pam was something special for she had made love to me without me ever being inside of her.

"Are you okay Michael?" my mother yelled from downstairs

"I'm fine mom."

"Okay."

Until I met my next crush, it was Pam that quenched my sexual desire. She was all that I wanted, thought about, dreamt about and hoped for. She would join me in my bedroom and satisfy me many times without ever stepping foot into my house. She was certainly special.

Chapter 23

Senior Year Finale'

THE YEAR WAS 1985 AND Ronald Regan was elected to four more years in the White House; Reaganomics was in full affect. In the meantime, I was failing English Twelve. It just so happened to be my first period class which for someone who had just finished an eight-hour shift three hours prior was probably the worse time of day it could have been.

I didn't care for English in the first place and the fact that I was sleepy didn't help matters much. I had to be awakened often, by both fellow students and the teacher. There was no way that I could work the hours that I was working and pass Senior English; just no way. The class was too demanding with the book reports and term papers we had to do which were half of your final grade.

I think the teacher wanted to pass me, but I wasn't completing any of her assignments. I tried, but just didn't have the time or energy. In retrospect, maybe if I had gone to her and told her what was going on with me, then maybe she would have understood and had some leniency, but I was and had never been the type of person to have someone show me special treatment or to feel sorry for me. It was my situation and I had to deal with it on my own.

As my birthday passed, I was nineteen and still in school. There were only three months left before graduation and everyone was making plans for their future, such as college, jobs, etc., but I was still clueless as to what I would be doing. Would I be working at The Commercial Appeal for minimum wage the rest of my life?

Michael Cavicante

There was a new Assistant Principal who had taken a liking to me. His name was Mr. Penn; he was a big, tall, black man. I guess he saw a lot of potential in me and knew that I was going through a lot at home. I never told him, but I guess he just sensed that all wasn't right with me.

HERE I AM IN A SENIOR YEAR PHOTO WHILE IN A
"JOBS FOR HIGH SCHOOL GRADUATES" CLASS

Maybe he could see the tiredness all over my face. Whatever it was that he picked up on, we sat and talked during my lunch breaks. I never shared with him what my father had done to me, but I did tell him a lot of other things. He really did have an interest in my well-being and became sort of like a father figure.

In the meantime—it was April and the Annual Junior Mister Contest was upon us. It was a contest in which male juniors and seniors dressed up like women and performed on stage. I was becoming more and more daring as time went by, so I decided to enter the contest. I would be Tina Turner. For once, I wanted to do something fun and exciting, so I prepared for it.

A Father's Double Life

For my costume, it was simple. I wore my mother's clothes which included one of her dresses, high heels and even a bra stuffed with toilet paper. I even borrowed one of her blonde wigs. Yes! I had finally figured out how she was able to remove her hair.

Though my grades were far from perfect, I was becoming somewhat of a perfectionist. I wanted everything and anything that I did to be right and wasn't going to accept mediocrity.

I rehearsed for hours on end while singing and making sure that my words where in sync with the instrumental version of the song that I would be singing. If I missed a cue by half a second, I would start over until I had it down perfectly. I was becoming obsessed with perfection. I guess I figured if I did everything in life one hundred percent the right way from there on out, then I wouldn't end up in the financial predicament that my parents found themselves. I was determined at a young age to do better with my life.

The day came and I was announced on stage. My practice paid off and I performed flawlessly while singing Tina Turner's *"Private Dancer."* I heard the student body laughing while I put on a show and had an absolute ball! I certainly had the legs to pull off a Tina Turner routine because they were certainly toned and I'm not a hairy person, so my legs looked silky smooth. I used to be asked in the football locker room if I shaved my legs which I didn't. That's just how hairless they appeared.

But even with my flawless performance and shapely legs, I didn't win. The contest was a combination of who looked most like a woman and also sounded good; I was neither. My broad shoulders, huge hands and facial hair, along with a voice unable of carrying a tune probably played a part in that, so the only thing flawless about the act was singing the lyrics.

Even more so, it was a popularity contest, so it would the most popular person in the contest that would be crowned Junior Mister, 1985; it wasn't me. Regardless of the outcome, I had a blast.

The month of May arrived shortly thereafter and by that time, I knew I had in fact failed twelfth grade English but had acquired the eighteen credits required for graduation and therefore could march during Pomp and Circumstance. I still had hopes that my English Teacher would pass me because I didn't want to have to attend summer school to make up the required class.

I was about to put my high school years behind me. During those years, I had been a member of the track team in which I threw the shot put, the wrestling team and the football team which I lettered in. Who knows what could have been had I been given the chance for a normal childhood. Coach David was the football coach for the '81-'82 Oakhaven Football Season, and therefore, I would have been playing tight-end, at least as a second stringer since Frog would have been a senior, but thanks to my dad, I was in foster homes that year and never had that opportunity.

I even went out for baseball and could hit the baseball a mile, but slung my bat, which meant that after I swung, whether I hit the ball or not, the bat went flying out of my hands towards first base as I batted left handed. My baseball pursuit would end after swinging my bat one day at practice and hitting the coach who just so happened to be the same coach of the football team, Coach Woody. After hitting him, he cut me from the team.

While thinking about what might have been, graduation night was upon me and my dad let me use his car, which was an orange, 1977 Chevy Monte Carlo. My mother had flown to Los Angeles several weeks prior and would miss the event. She was to care for her mother who was battling colon cancer, but my father was there.

The Senior Class

of

Oakhaven High School

announces its

Commencement Exercises

Wednesday evening, May twenty-ninth

Nineteen hundred eighty-five

eight o'clock

Oakhaven High School Auditorium

Memphis, Tennessee

OFFICIAL INVITATION ANNOUNCEMENT FOR
MY HIGH SCHOOL GRADUATION

A Father's Double Life

I sat in the front of the auditorium along with the other graduates and listened as the Jaime, the Valedictorian speak, as the ceremony continued. I sat there thinking to myself,

"That guy is going to be rich and very successful."

I then thought to myself,

"I graduated number 78 out of 82 graduates." as we had received our final class rankings just days before graduation. I felt like a complete dumb ass.

I knew that I went through a lot, but I didn't want to use those things as an excuse as to why I failed. I knew school was important so why did I put my job and working ahead of my schooling? The only consolation I had was that I wasn't ranked number eighty-two.

As I peered around at my senior classmates that sat amongst me; I wondered to whom that dishonorable distinction would belong to. At least it wasn't me.

Was that supposed to make me feel better? I then wondered,

"What if number eighty-two went through the same things that I did as a kid, or perhaps, even worse? It really didn't matter at that point. I couldn't turn back the hands of time; I couldn't erase the past; I couldn't undo what had already been done; it happened and was now behind me. I was only nineteen and I had the rest of my life ahead of me."

While sitting there pondering those thoughts, I had to be nudged to stand up because it was time to march on stage in order to get our diplomas, while the music played. I watched while the first several students were handed scrolls.

"How am I going to get my Diploma if I didn't pass English 12? This is going to be really embarrassing if I am not handed a scroll." I thought to myself in anxiety.

As it turned out, I was handed a scroll.

"Thank God! Whew." I said to myself while walking across the stage.

After getting back to our seats, I realized that the scroll was just a blank piece of paper; it was just for show. Shortly thereafter, the ceremony was over and we were released. I then located my dad in the crowd and we exited the auditorium. After getting outside, he congratulated me with a brief hug and a tear or two actually came from his eyes as he told me to have a good time. He rode home with Doris our neighbor, who also attended.

Michael Cavicante

GRADUATION DAY WITH MY FATHER
AND NEXT DOOR NEIGHBORS

I didn't have a girlfriend, so a couple of football players and I just hung out. We just drove around for the most part. We didn't go to any parties, clubs or anything. It was actually a pretty boring night, so it wasn't long before I was dropping them off and went home.

Within days, I got my final report card in the mail. It was official; I had in fact failed English and would have to attend summer school in order to get my Diploma. I enrolled at a nearby high school and would be taking the dreaded class from twelve-noon until three which was perfect. It meant that I could work at night, go home and get enough sleep to be ready for school.

MY HIGH SCHOOL SENIOR HEAD

Chapter 24

Summer School

IN THE SUMMER OF 1985, I would attend a record fifth high school. I don't know if it was a record or not, but it was my personal record. That high school would be Hamilton. It was one of the most sought after high schools in South Memphis; probably because they were perennial powerhouses in both basketball and football while playing at the Triple-A level. Oakhaven was Double-A.

At Hamilton, I met Tonya. She was a black girl of cinnamon-brown complexion, slender, standing five-foot three and simply adorable. She talked with an extreme southern drawl, which made her even more attractive to me. Showing immediate interest in me, she asked me out of the blue one day to carry her books which I did gladly. We had immediate chemistry and talked openly and freely about a variety of anything and everything. She thought I was extremely smart and wondered why I was in summer school, but after I explained it to her, she understood. I thought she was equally as bright.

We went out a couple of times which included visiting historic Beale Street. The landmark had been around for over a hundred years, but in months prior to my visit, it had received a much-needed facelift. I had been working right down the street, but had never visited the district. I must say that I was pleasantly surprised.

Michael Cavicante

HISTORICAL BEALE STREET IN DOWNTOWN MEMPHIS

It was a short stretch of road extending maybe a block or two and was blocked off at each end to prohibit automobile traffic. As we walked down the middle of the street hand-in-hand, we enjoyed live music and the festive atmosphere as a whole. It was the first time I had been on a real date, so for me, the night was really special. We grabbed a bite to eat and I took her back home.

After arriving at her house, I walked her to the door, gave her a soft kiss on the cheek and said goodnight, after which, I felt like she was expecting me to do something different, but I didn't have a clue as to what. Tonya and I would go out a couple of more times without me ever suggesting sex in any way, shape or form. We would, after only a couple of weeks stop seeing each other. I was really hurt by it because I had met her mother who was very classy, literally, as that was her first name, Classie. Tonya herself should have been from Georgia, because she was an absolute peach. I was definitely falling for her.

Fortunately for me, there would be others that wanted to be with me, in particular, Jean and Mary. They were two other girls I also met in summer school. They actually fought over me (not literally), but talked about which one would have me. It was no competition as far as I was concerned. Jean was hands-down the better choice. She had style, intelligence and was a lot better looking. I visited Jean a couple of times and we grew to be really good friends over the next couple of months.

It was easy for me to see that girls liked me, but somewhere, I was totally missing the boat. I just never knew how to move into a relationship. These were just good, old-fashioned, southern girls, so I guess they wanted a guy who knew what to do and how to take charge. I was not that guy.

Then there was Joyce. I actually don't remember how we met her, but she lived close to my job, so maybe that had something to do with it. She was twenty-two years old and like the others, she was the bomb. She had two kids, one of which was born with trisomy G.

I thought we would be the perfect fit since my brother was also mentally slow, so I knew how to deal with the situation.

She was slender, light-skinned and very attractive. She called me and asked me to come see her on occasions. When visiting her, I could tell that she was downright crazy about me and I must admit that I was crazy as hell about her also. I liked her so much that I told my mother about her over the phone. Yes, she was still in California tending to her mother, but for some reason my mother didn't approve of Joyce, so I eventually left her alone. I don't think my mother was pleased about the fact that she had two kids, but I didn't care, she could have had ten, I would have still adored her.

Here I was, a healthy, young, virile and compassionate young man just wanting to be loved, and better yet, wanting to love.

Well, if there was ever a girl that was willing to show me love, it was acne-faced Sheila. After arriving at work one night, I discovered that she had been hired to work as a casual. Do you remember her? She was the girl I met while attending Northside who wrote Beef Cake on my butt, not to mention giving me a case of the *"Blue Balls"*. Yep, she was working at The Commercial Appeal with me. I couldn't believe it.

She went crazy when she saw me as I thought,

"Oh my God."

I was glad to see her, but knew that I didn't want a relationship with her. I had been complimented on my eyes, physique, personality and charm, so I guess by that point in my life, I knew that I could have my pick of the litter and didn't have to settle for the likes of her. Yeah, just like the majority of society, I had become superficial. I knew that Sheila was a beautiful person on the inside, but still, I wanted no part of her. I wanted my Pam.

If it sounds like I had the so-called big-head or was conceited, trust me, I really wasn't, and never have been. I was just at the point in my life where I felt like I could do better, that's all.

Even though I consistently shunned her, she made it known to every person at work that she wanted to be with me and literally followed me everywhere while at work. She was totally obsessed with me.

Other women at work thought it was cute, but I felt smothered. Every time I turned around, there she was. I still liked her as a person, but that was about it. Her pursuit of me continued throughout the summer. Thankfully, I usually only saw her on Saturday nights.

As far as Summer School, I breezed through with no problem and finally passed English Twelve with a B average. After attending eleven different schools in thirteen years, I finally received my diploma in mid-August via mail. It was time to make a decision about my future.

Chapter 25

Career Decision

I don't know what actually propelled me to pursue the military, but for whatever reason, I did. So one day in mid-August, I went down to see a recruiter in Whitehaven. All of the branches of service were in one building, but I went directly to the Air Force Recruiter's office.

I was familiar with Vietnam and realized that the Army and Marines were the two branches of service that were in the most danger during wartime because they were normally the first to be called, not to mention on the field of battle. Yeah, I was finally starting to acquire some common sense.

As I walked into the office, I was greeted by a white man.
"Hello, how are you doing?"
"Hello sir."
"How may I help you?"
"I'd like to see about joining the Air Force."
"Okay, have you taken the ASVAB?"
"No sir."
"Do you have a high school diploma?"
"Yes sir."
"Okay, but before taking the ASVAB, you have to take a screening test. Do you have time?"
"Yes sir."

He then pulled out a pencil and test pamphlet, gave it to me and told me to begin. While taking the exam, I thought it was pretty easy and in

Michael Cavicante

less than an hour, I handed the test back to him. After taking about five minutes to grade it, he responded,

"Very good."

"How did I do sir?"

"You answered 46 of 48 correctly."

"Cool, what now sir?"

"Well, we aren't accepting any enlistees right now. I will call you when we are."

"Okay sir."

While walking away from his station, I wondered why he even had me take the test in the first place and came to the conclusion that he probably didn't think I would pass anyway. He just wanted to see how poorly I was going to do. Well, I surely fooled him.

I was disappointed and wondered what I would do, but as I continued through the maze of offices and walked towards the exit, a man in a Navy Uniform stopped me.

"Would you like to join the Navy?"

"Nah….I don't think so sir," I said, while shaking my head.

"Why not?"

"I don't know. I had my heart set on the Air Force."

"The Air Force? The Navy is better. Come sit down with me and I'll tell you why."

"Okay."

"What's your name young man?"

"Michael."

"My name is Art."

We then sat down at his desk. He was so enthusiastic, how could I not go over and talk to him? After listening to him for just five minutes, he had me sold. He made the Navy sound so great while telling me about all of the places he had been and everything that he had done, it was impossible to tell him no.

"So, do you want to join Michael?"

"Yes Sir."

"Okay, so you have to take a screening test."

"I already took one sir."

"You did, when?"

"Over at the Air Force Recruiting Office."

"How did you do?"

"I got 46 of 48 correct."

184

"You are shittin' me."

"Huh?"

"That is fantastic!"

I sat there and watched while Art scurried over to the Air Force Recruiter's Office and within seconds, he was back.

"Okay; you're good to go."

"I don't have to take another one?"

"Nope, you are just fine. So when do you want to take the ASVAB?"

"I can take it whenever you want me to, sir."

"You certainly have that Sir thing down pat."

"My mother always told me to address my elders as Sir or Ma'm, sir."

"Your mother did a great job."

"Okay, we're going to set you up for the ASVAB in a couple of days. It will be given at the MEPS Station downtown at seven o'clock. I will pick you up, okay?"

"Okay, sir." I said as I stood up and shook his hand.

After a few days, it would figure that the test would be given on a morning after I had labored all night, at seven o'clock. Nonetheless, I got off of work, went home and took a shower. My recruiter picked me up promptly at six-thirty and took me to the MEPS Station. M.E.P.S. stands for Military Entrance Processing Station.

I arrived at six-fifty and seemingly, was wide-awake. I walked into the school-like classroom and sat down with about ten other people. The facilitator gave us instructions and how each part of the test was to be timed; afterwards, the three-hour exam began.

I was excited as the test started because if it was anything like the screening test then I knew that I was going to blow it away, but it seemed like every time a section of the test was over, I had to be awakened because I was nodding on and off during the whole quiz.

Before I knew it, the clock struck ten, the test was over and I was convinced that I had failed it. It seemed that I had slept through at least half of it, but at that point, I was tired and just wanted to go home. My recruiter picked me up and while driving, he asked,

"So how do you think you did?"

"I don't know sir, I kept falling asleep."

"Well, we'll see. I'm sure you did okay."

"Then you have more confidence in me than I do."

"Anybody who gets 46 of 48 correct on the screening test, I've got to feel pretty good about it."

"I guess."

"I'm sure you did fine Michael."

A part of me didn't even care anymore. I had a massive headache, was exhausted and just wanted to sleep.

After being dropped off, I went into the house and passed out on the floor in front of the television and slept for hours.

When I finally awakened, I propped myself up with my left hand while looking around the room. My dad was sitting in his customary spot on the couch smoking a cigarette.

"Did my recruiter call dad, " I asked, while rubbing my eyes.

"No, nobody called for you," he replied, while exhaling his smoke.

"I've got to call him. What time is it?"

"Four thirty."

"Four thirty? I've got to call him."

I got up, located the phone, pulled out Art's business card and dialed his number.

"Navy Recruiting Office, Art speaking."

"Hello Art, this is Michael Cavicante. I was calling to see how I did on the ASVAB."

"Mike, you got over like a fat rat."

"Huh? Say that again?"

"You passed; you scored a fifty-three. You're in."

"A fifty-three, is that all?"

"Listen, the average score is thirty-two and you scored a fifty-three."

"That sucks." I replied.

"You told me yourself you fell asleep on half the test and you still scored a fifty-three, so be happy." He said.

"I guess."

"Okay Michael, I will call you tomorrow and we will set up the next step, okay?"

"Okay sir."

"Mike; please call me Art, okay?"

"Yes, sir, I mean okay Sir Art. I mean, Art Sir."

"Bye Michael."

"Bye."

The call ended as we both hung up.

A Father's Double Life

Of course I related a fifty-three to being an "F" like in school, but those tests were scored very differently, so a fifty-three was in fact, considered a decent score. I still wasn't happy with it, but I had passed, which at the time was good enough for me.

My score of 53 represented my AFQT, which stood for Armed Forces Qualification Standard. It meant that I scored higher than 53% of all test-takers in my age group. The score required to pass was a 31 at the time, so I had in fact done really well, even if I did fall asleep.

After hanging up the phone and at that very instant, it had sunk in that I was going into the Navy. I then jumped for joy.

"Dad, I'm going into the Navy."

"Really, when are you leaving?" as he extinguished his cigarette

"I don't know yet, but soon, I think."

"Well, one thing about the military. It's either going to make you or break you."

He stood up and asked me,

"Come here son."

I walked over to him and he gave me a hug which was very uncommon. Next to my high school graduation, I couldn't remember the last time I received one from him. He stepped back and looked me in the face.

"I am proud of you son. I know you have never heard me say it, but I am. I put you through a lot, I put this family through a lot and I'm sorry, okay?"

"Okay dad."

I then hugged him.

"I love you dad."

"I love you too son." He replied as tears came to his eyes.

For the first time in my life, he told me that he was proud of me and loved me. We called my mother who was still in Los Angeles caring for her mother.

"Hello mom."

"Oh... hey; how you doing son?"

"I'm okay."

"What's up?"

"How's your mother?" I asked

"She's going to be okay. They removed part of her colon and got the cancer."

"Well that's good."

"How are you doing son? I'm sorry I missed your graduation."

"Don't worry mom, I understand."
"Did your father show up?"
"Yes, he was there."
"He better had been. He doesn't do anything for you."
"Yeah, I know." I answered, as he was standing right in front of me looking in my face.
"I'm always letting you down son." my mother replied.
"No you're not; you're always there for me. I've got something to tell you."
"What son? What?"
"I'm going into the Navy."
"You're going in the Navy?"
"Yes mother."
"Why."
"I have to try and make a better life for myself."
"But why the Navy?"
"Because the Air Force wasn't taking enlistees."
"No; why the military?"
"I know what you meant; I was just trying to be funny. I don't know mom, it just seems like my only option. I have to start living for me."
"Well I can certainly understand that. When are you leaving?"
"I don't know, but probably soon."
"How soon?"
"Hopefully within the next month."
"Are you serious? I have to get home."
"What about your mother?"
"She will be okay. I got to get back home to see my baby boy off."
"That would be nice."
"Well, I'm behind whatever decision you make son. I'm proud of you."
"Thanks mom."
"Okay honey, I'll be home as soon as I can. I love you."
"Love you too mom, bye."
"Bye son."
I then hung up the phone.
"What did your mother say?" my father asked.
"That she was proud of me and she's on her way home."
"Good, it's about time she got back."
The next step was to take a physical exam, so my recruiter picked me

up the next day and took me back to the MEPS Station. While on the way, he asked,

"So Michael, do you know how to swim?"

"Yes sir."

"Well that's good, because if you're going to be in the Navy, you have to be able to swim."

"Yes sir."

At that very moment, I remembered what my mother had repeatedly told me over the last nineteen years of my life and that was,

"My son, everything happens for a reason."

I thought about almost losing my life as a child when I was pushed into the deep end of the pool. If not for that day, I probably would've never learned how to swim.

"God has a path for all of us my son. He makes no mistakes." she would tell me.

So with those words, I guess it was meant for me to go into the Navy.

After arriving at the MEPS Station, I was medically interviewed by an oriental Physician who had a smile on his face from the first moment he laid eyes on me. He asked me some medical questions and then sent me to another room. When arriving there, I was asked to strip down and to step behind a curtain. After doing so, that same doctor that had just interviewed me was still smiling and asked me to bend over.

He had plastic gloves on and after I bent down, I felt his finger go into my butt. It felt very uncomfortable, but he was done quickly. I found out later that he was checking for a swollen prostate. At that very point, I thought to myself as to how in the world could any man be gay. That was just a finger and it hurt and he had a lubricant on the glove.

I didn't know if he was queer or not, but I had a pretty robust rear-end. Because of that, I would have some weird experiences in my life. Maybe it also had something to do with my father's affection for me.

I then went into another room with a bunch of other guys. While sitting on the floor, legs fully extended, straight out in front of us, we had to touch our toes which was no problem for me. I had passed all phases of the physical and was ready to see my career counselor the next day in order to pick a job.

But before I left the MEPS station that morning, I met Candace. She was a four-foot eleven, dark-skinned, black girl that might have weighed

Michael Cavicante

ninety-five pounds, soaked and wet, but had a nice little frame on her. She was kind of shy, but said hello to me anyway.

We talked briefly and found out that we had something in common. Candace was seventeen and living in a foster home. I don't know why she was at the MEPS Station, because she never went into the military. After asking for her phone number, she gave it to me and we said good-bye.

The next day, I went to see my Career Counselor and sat down to discuss my options as far as a job in the Navy. He gave me a bunch of eight by eleven inch cards which had occupations and their description on them.

I initially chose Aviation Structural Mechanic, because I wanted to pick a skill and therefore a trade that I could use when I got out of the Navy, but I had to wait six months for that particular school to open up. As I continued going through this stack of cards, I found a job that said Boiler Technician, 6YO-ATF.

"What does 6YO-ATF stand for? I asked.

"It means that you have to obligate yourself for six years and also that you will be going into the Advanced Technical Field."

"Six Years. That's a long time. Do I qualify for this program?"

"With your score Michael, you have a wide variety of choices and yes you do qualify."

As I continued reading the card, it kept getting better.

"So I will be advanced to the rank of E-4 upon completion of my school?"

"Yep, and that's big, because you will be a Petty Officer before you even hit the fleet, which also means more privileges and less menial tasks to complete."

"Wow, okay."

I then read what would be the clincher.

"I will get twenty thousand dollars if I re-enlist?"

"Yes Michael, because the Boiler Technician is considered a critical rate, so you may get up to twenty thousand dollars for signing up again."

"What does critical mean?"

"It simply means that the Boiler Technician rating is in high demand right now and the Navy wants to retain them which is the reason for the bonus."

"Twenty thousand dollars? That is all I needed to hear. Sign me up. I'm done sir."

"Are you sure?"

"Yes sir. Absolutely! That is more money than I could ever know what to do with."

Of course, I had been poor my whole young life, so twenty thousand dollars sounded like an awful lot of money to me and since Boiler Technicians were in high demand there was no waiting period. It was Friday, August 23rd, but I had already worked twenty-four hours for the week and wanted to finish it out as Saturday was the last day of the pay period.

I told Art that I wanted to see one more payday before I left so that I could give my parents some money. We got paid on Wednesdays and the next payday would fall on the twenty-eighth, so I elected to leave on Thursday, the twenty-ninth. It was set. I took my oath soon thereafter.

I went around and told all the neighborhood kids when I was leaving. I also told all of the girls that I met that summer, especially Candy, the four-foot eleven gem that I met at the MEPS Station. Actually by that point, I had already called and visited a couple of times. She was so sweet. I had always been pretty lucky with meeting nice girls.

As I made preparations to leave, I realized that I only had one week left in Memphis, Tennessee. I was so excited—that was until it dawned on me as to how I would be getting to Basic Training. Boot Camp would was in Great Lakes, Illinois, just outside of Chicago.

I was told Monday, August 26th, that I would be flying to Chicago's O'Hare Airport. I absolutely freaked; I wasn't getting on a plane! There had been flights going down like crazy that year and I wasn't about to become a casualty.

On June 23rd, 1985, an Air India Flight 182 blew up at 31,000 ft, killing 329 people. On August 2nd, Delta Flight 191 crashed killing 137 and most recently at that time, on August 12th, Japan Flight 123 crashed, killing 520 people. No sir, I was not getting on a plane that year or any other year; no way, no how; I was a frantic and going nuts when I called my recruiter.

"Naval Recruiting District Memphis, Art speaking"

"Hello Art, this is Michael Cavicante; Can you please drive me to Great Lakes?"

"Why?"

"I'm not getting on a plane."

"Why not?"

"Why not? Haven't you heard? Planes are going down and blowing up like crazy."

"Michael, do you know the odds of that happening?"

"Obviously pretty high; I am not getting on a plane."

"Mike, if you're going to go into the military, you need to get used to flying."

"I'm sorry Art, but I'm too young to die. You're not getting me on no plane."

"We still have a couple of days. I will come over and see you in person, okay?"

"Yes sir."

"Alright then—good-bye."

"Good-bye, sir."

That very same day, my mother returned from Los Angeles. She was ecstatic to see me and I guess the feelings were mutual because I was also very happy to see her. She greeted me with a customary hug and smothered me with kisses while she spoke,

"My precious son; so you're going into the Army."

"Huh, I'm going into the Navy, but I might not be leaving."

"Why not?"

"Do you know how I will be getting to boot camp?"

"By plane I guess."

"That's right mom, by plane. I am not getting on a plane. They are dangerous."

"Why do you say that?"

"Gosh, does anyone around here watch the news? Planes are going down left and right; people are being killed."

"Michael, you've been on a plane before."

"Yeah I know, but I was only three years old. I didn't know any better back then, nor do I remember it. I know better now and I am not getting on a plane."

She then sat me down and talked to me.

"Michael, do you believe in God?"

"Of course I do."

"Then son, put your life in his hands. Look at everything that you have been through. For Christ's sake Michael, you walked thirty miles in the middle of the night; you rode your bike on the interstate on flat tires in a torrential rainstorm, you took your dad's car out in the middle of the night and drove a hundred miles per hour. You are an angel and a *survivor. God isn't going to allow anything to happen to you. Put your faith in him son and you will continue to be protected, okay sweetheart? So you get on that plane and go into the Marines, okay?*

"I'm going into the Navy mom."

"Navy, Marines, whatever, you just go and make a better life for yourself, okay?

"Okay mom," as she pulled me close and hugged me again.

With her motherly words, I had calmed down and was ready for my new journey. Over the next couple of days, I said my final goodbyes to everybody. The sweetest good-bye was from Candace. I went to visit her and she was adorable, but could never look me in the eyes. We had talked on the phone a couple of more times prior to that good-bye and she had really fallen for me which was evident by the way she hugged me, because she didn't want to let me go. She was the last girl I saw before heading to Boot Camp.

I got paid on Wednesday, August 28th and gave my last check from The Commercial Appeal to my parents, but kept a couple of dollars out for the trip.

The following day, on the 29th of August, 1985, my recruiter picked me up from my house as my family and neighborhood friends stood around outside and said their good-byes.

My mother cried while both parents and siblings hugged me.

"Have a good time in the Army," my mother said.

"Mom, for the last time, I'm going into the Navy."

"Navy, Army, whatever; just take care of yourself baby."

"Okay mom."

"Robin was as tall, as big and as strong as I was, but I never realized how much until he gave me his version of the Bear Hug.

"Give me hug little brother," he said.

I walked over to him and he lifted me in the air with both arms tightly around my body and squeezed the living crap of me. He squeezed me so hard, I could hardly breathe.

"Ro—bin. Let—me—down." as I struggled to speak.

He then dropped me on my feet and I shook my head in disbelief.

"I didn't realize you were so strong," as he then snickered.

I then walked over to my baby sister and her eyes were full of tears.

"Are you okay Wendy?"

"I'm going to miss you Michael. Are you ever coming back?" as she looked up into my eyes

"I'll be back to visit."
"When?"
"I don't know."
"Awe—I love you Michael. I don't want you to go."
"I know, Wendy, I love you too, but I have to go, okay?"
"Awe, okay. Bye Michael."
"Bye, Wendy."

What would a good-bye be without saying so long to Willie? He was the brother that I really didn't have. He was there for me when no one else was. In a way, next to God, he was my Guardian Angel. What would my childhood have been if not for Willie?

They say that true friends only come around once in a lifetime. Well my friendship with Willie would certainly solidify that statement; he was a true friend. We had a bond that was unbreakable and that would be forged for all of eternity. He knew it, I knew it and without anything to be said, we gave each other a short glare; only a hug was needed.

"I love you man," Willie said as we embraced.

"I love you too," I reciprocated.

I then grabbed my duffle bag and walked to my recruiter's car as he waited with the passenger door open. With my loved ones waving good-bye, the car backed out of the driveway leaving only a cloud of dust behind as I then rode off into the sunset to begin a new life.

Chapter 26
Bon Voyage

After arriving at Memphis International Airport, my recruiter took me to the airline counter and got my one-way ticket to Great Lakes. He then walked me to my gate and gave me instructions on what to do when I arrived in Chicago. He then left my sight, never to be heard from, or seen by my eyes again.

After taking a seat while knowing that I had finally broken away from a life of hurt and disappointment, I became very emotional and started crying and the crying got worse while I sobbed uncontrollably when another young black guy came over to me.

"Yo brother, are you okay?" he inquired as I looked up at him.
"Yeah, I'm okay," I replied, as he sat next to me.
"What's wrong dude?"
"Nothing, I'm just really messed up right now."
"What's your name?"
"Michael."
"My name is Clarence."
"Hello Clarence."
"Are you on your way to Navy Boot Camp?"
"Yeah."
"Me too."

We then heard the final call to board the plane.

"Come on Mike, let's go man." he said as he put his hand on my shoulder.

We then got up, got in line, pulled out our boarding passes and identification as I was still crying. After being checked, we boarded the plane and took our seats. We just so happened to be sitting right next to each other.

The cabin doors closed, the plane soon thereafter backed up and I only began to cry harder, not only for the emotions I was feeling, but realized that I was really on a plane, a plane that could crash or blow up and kill me. To make matters worse, that darn flight attendant was giving us instructions on what to do if the plane went down. That was the last thing that I needed to see and then thought to myself,

"Why would she be doing that? Why would she be preparing us to crash if the odds were so great that more than likely, we wouldn't?"

My mother's words had gotten me that far, but I was now at the point of no return. I felt helpless and while the plane taxied the runway, I talked to myself;

"I'm going to die, I'm going to die," and I started to cry even more.

Clarence then grabbed and held my hand. I must say that I felt uncomfortable about him holding my hand and said to myself,

"Oh my gosh, another tuity-fruity. Maybe you need to be introduced to my dad. You guys would get along just great." But I was so cathartic I just let it be.

I then felt the thrust of the plane as the back of my head was forced against the seat as the plane sped up to take-off. I looked out of the window and watched the ground zoom by as the plane lifted off the runway and we became airborne. I watched as buildings, automobiles and houses got smaller while the plane ascended higher and higher.

It then made this big U-turn. I just knew we were dead and was balling big time. The plane finally steadied and stayed straight, but I continued to cry. Then the Captain came over the intercom and announced that we were at a cruising altitude of thirty-two thousand feet. After doing some quick math in my head which I was really good at, I realized that we were six doggone miles above land and my crying picked up again.

"Six miles up in the air, ain't nobody surviving no crash," I thought to myself.

My ears all of a sudden seemingly lost their hearing as the noise level dropped at least forty decibels.

"What is wrong with my ears? I just lost my freaking hearing."

"It's perfectly normal. It just happens," Clarence responded.

"Why do they do that?"

A Father's Double Life

"*I don't know; it just happens.*"

After about ten more minutes, my tears finally went away and I relaxed. As I relaxed, I looked out of the window and came to realize how smooth the plane ride was. I watched the clouds beneath as they resembled gigantic balls of cotton. It seemed like all of a sudden my fear had gone away. That was until the plane started shaking badly.

"*What wrong? What's going on?*" I said.

"*It's just a little turbulence,*" Clarence replied.

"*Turbulence? What's that?*"

"*I don't know; I just know it happens at times.*"

"*How can this idiot be so calm about stuff, when he doesn't even know how or why they are happening?*" I thought, but then said,

"*How can you be so calm when you don't even know what it is?*"

"*All I know is that it's perfectly normal.*"

"*Nothing is normal about how my ears feel and nothing is normal about the way this plane is shaking,*" I said as I looked around the cabin and saw everyone else at ease.

I was getting ready to start crying again, but the trembling of the plane finally went away and I was all right. My calmness remained for the rest of the flight; that was until we landed.

The seat belt light came on, but mine had been buckled the whole time anyway. I looked out the window while the plane descended. As we got closer to the runway, I realized just how fast that plane was going because there were points of reference while I watched trees and other scenery zoom by the window.

"*How in the heck is this plane going to be able to stop?*" I thought.

I felt the landing gear hit the runway and it seemed as if the plane was going three hundred miles an hour.

"*Oh my gosh, we're going to crash. This stupid plane isn't slowing down,*" I pondered.

But then I heard the loud winding roar of the engine and observed the wings as the hydraulic flaps dropped to break the wind flow across the wing itself. The plane slowed from doing three hundred miles an hour all the way down to a snails crawl. I was finally safe and had endured my first memorable plane ride. Outside of the turbulence, it was actually pretty nice. It would have been a lot nicer had I not cried half the way there.

It was around four in the afternoon when the plane took its resting place at the gate. I heard the cabin door open and my ears suddenly felt normal again; however I was speechless upon departure. I had never traveled by myself before and certainly wasn't ready for something like O'Hare Airport. I was in complete awe when we stepped into the terminal. I had never seen so many people in one place. It was quite overwhelming, but Clarence led me through the airport, and no, he wasn't holding my hand any longer. Thank goodness.

We found our way to baggage claim, got our bags and then looked for the bus that would take us to Recruit Training Command, Great Lakes or, RTC for short.

After locating the bus, I found that there were others already onboard when we embarked. We took a seat and waited for the rest of the recruits to get on. There was a roll call and after everyone was accounted for as we then left for Boot Camp.

After about a forty-five minute ride, we arrived at the Naval Base. Clarence and I stayed close together while exiting the bus and into a building. After getting inside, we were issued a blanket, a pillowcase and a couple of sheets. We were also given what were called chits. They were vouchers that allowed us to buy supplies until we got our first paycheck; that would be a ways off. We were then marched to another building where we would spend the night; it was only seven o'clock. When the night was all said and done, eighty-two young men were about to start a new life as we slept in bunks in this one big room.

I barely slept all night because I was too busy thinking about what my future would hold and if I had made the right decision. My tossing and turning didn't help matters and the night flew by. Two Navy guys awakened us at five the next morning. They would be our mama and daddy for the next nine weeks. Boot Camp was eight weeks, but one week was allowed for processing. They were referred to as the P-Days.

The two guys that so rudely awoke us were called Company Commanders or CC's for short. Their titles and names were UT1 Albright and BM1 Murtaugh.

The bright lights came on and while being blinded, I heard what sounded like someone beating on a metal trashcan. I then heard a voice say,

"On your feet, on your feet sailors, you're in the Navy now! Stand at attention in front of your racks! If you don't know what a rack is, I'm referring to your bunks! If you don't know what a bunk is, I'm referring to your bed! If you don't know what a bed is, then God help you!"

A Father's Double Life

They gave us our instructions as to what the day would consist of, which included breakfast, supplies, haircuts and clothing issue.

I will refer to the Company Commanders as BM1 and UT1 for short. UT1 meant that one of the Company Commanders was a Utilities Man, First Class Petty Officer. BM1 was a Boatswains Mate, First Class Petty Officer. You will hear UT1 predominantly more because he was the lead Company Commander and the hard-ass between the two.

After getting dressed, we marched out and to the chow hall. I must say the food was pretty good and by the way, I entered Boot Camp at six-foot one, two hundred fifty-four pounds and just like on my high school football team, I was the biggest guy in the company. Everybody was quiet during chow and not really saying a whole lot. I think we were all kind of shell-shocked.

After breakfast, we marched to the Navy Exchange and were given a net bag which would be our dirty laundry bag, but on that day, it would be used to hold personal effects that we bought with the chits that he had been given the day before.

We were instructed by our Company Commanders on exactly what to buy. We purchased such items as black and white stenciling pencils, toothbrush, toothbrush holder, toothpaste, soap, soap dish, shaving cream and razors. Those items would be our only items for the next two months.

After our visit to the Navy Exchange, we stood in line for haircuts. My hair was already short, so it wasn't a big deal to me. I can't say the same for some of the others, especially some of the Caucasian and Hispanic guys who had really long hair. A couple of them actually cried after their hair was shaved off.

It was going on twelve noon and time for lunch, so we marched back to the chow hall. Man, that food sure was good! After lunch, we marched to clothing issue. We were given these big green duffle bags and in those bags, we would put our uniforms. It was an all day affair as we sat in a building called a hangar. If you ever saw the movie, *"An Officer and a Gentleman,"* the building resembled the same one that Richard Gere and Lou Gossett Jr. fought in near the end of the movie.

There was no air-conditioning and what resembled big garage doors were left open. It was very hot in Great Lakes and must have been over a hundred degrees that day. I sat there hanging my head while we rotated eighty-two young men waited their turn to be measured and issued the next set of GI GEAR. GI stands government issue.

As I hung my head and stared at the floor, I watched sweat drip off of my brow and into a small puddle beneath me, at which point I asked myself,

"What in the hell have I gotten myself into?"

I surely thought I had made a mistake by joining the military, but then thought again as to what very few options I actually had at the time; the answer was

"None."

So I sucked it up and told myself that no matter what, I was going to make the best of it.

The day continued and when it was over, we were issued four sets of dungarees, two sets of working whites, two sets of working blues, two sets of dress whites, one set of dress blues, one pair of boon-dockers (boots), one pair of dress shoes, six t-shirts, six pair of tighty-whities, six pair of white socks, six pair of dress socks, five Dixie Cups (navy hats), a black web belt, two white web belts, two belt buckles and a knit cap. That would conclude the clothing issue. Guess what we had to do next? You'll find out.

After a very long day, we went to dinner and then headed back to the building where we had spent our first couple of nights. We were in bed early again at eight o'clock.

The next morning we were marched to breakfast and then to medical. Over the next several days, we had medical records set up and were given a variety of shots, such as flu, tetanus, etc. We then went to lunch and back to the barracks. Afterwards, we spent the rest of the day stenciling all of those clothes that we had gotten the day before.

Until that point in my life, I loved my last name — CAVICANTE. It was unique, it was different, it was special and it was original. Well, over the course of the next four hours, I grew to hate my name because it had to be stenciled onto all of my clothing.

We used pre-cut stencil boards that already had our last names on them and for the next four hours, we traced out our names onto our clothes. Yes, at least for that particular day, I hated the name CAVICANTE with a passion. I had wished it were Jones or Smith, or better yet, Me. Anything but CAVICANTE, but after I finished with the grueling, tedious task, I was proud to see my name appear on the clothing.

We went to dinner later that evening and then back to the barracks. The next morning, we were instructed to pack all of our clothing, along with our personal items in that big green duffle bag. The only things left out were a set of dungarees which were the equivalent to blue jeans, but had bell-bottoms; a long-sleeve cotton blue shirt, a black web belt, one belt buckle, a pair of black dress socks, a pair of white socks, which we wore under the black ones, boon-dockers, and a black knit cap; all of which, we would wear that day and would be our uniform for the duration of boot camp. We were officially raisin-heads and would be for the first four weeks of basic training. I'll explain what raisin-heads means later.

We fell into ranks outside of the building with our duffle bags on our backs. We were then marched to our new home all the way on the other side of the base, while UT1 called out marching orders in relation to our feet striking the ground. He was the only one talking while we were on our way to what would be our home for the next two months.

"Your left, your left, your left, right, left," he repeated.

"Come on you slugs, get in step; it's not that hard!"

"Your left, your left, your left, right, left!"

"You guys are pathetic! Stay in step! Is this the ten thousand pounds of puppy shit that I inherited? Get your asses in gear."

"Your left, your left, your left, right, left!"

Outside of UT1 bashing us, those duffle bags started getting extremely heavy after only several blocks and I was a big, strong dude, so I can imagine how heavy it must have seemed to the smaller guys in the company, but we continued to march anyway. I'd say it had to be at least a mile before we finally arrived at the barracks that would be our home for the remainder of boot camp.

Over the next several days, the more sedate of the CC's, BM1, showed us how to store our belongings, how to fold our clothes and how to make our beds; they all had to be done a certain way. Of course, we all wouldn't get it the first time or even the second time. I am generally speaking for everyone else, because if you showed me once, more than likely, I had it. I was very quick to pick up on things and had an unquenchable desire for knowledge.

Each company was given a number and my company's number was 296 and pronounced, two-nine-six, not two hundred ninety-six. Company 295 was our sister company and located in the adjacent barracks just across the courtyard. **Processing was now complete!!**

Chapter 27

Flashbacks

Boot Camp officially started Saturday, September seventh. On the first day, certain people were assigned positions by UT1, but the RPOC is the only person I remember. RPOC was pronounced are-pock, and stood for (Recruit Petty Officer in Charge); his name was Robert. He was a sharp, white kid who stood about five-foot eight and was perfect for the job. He had Napoleon disorder.

The RPOC was in charge in the absence of the Company Commanders and also called the commands when we marched. Robert was as brilliant a young kid as any I had ever met and the right person assigned the position.

Again, I weighed in at two hundred fifty-four pounds and even though I had a lot of muscle-tone and didn't think I was fat, I was put on the so-called *"Fat Boy Program"*.

Being on that program meant that for the duration of boot camp, I would have to run two extra PT's (Physical Training) every week which included, a mile and a half run, fifty sit-ups, thirty push-ups, fifty jump-in jacks, etc.

At that point, I was still wondering if I had made the right decision, but I knew that I had to settle in and was determined to make the best of it. I made the following my motto;

"Make the best of and learn as much from whatever situation you are put into, no matter how short or long you may be in that situation. It will serve you positively in some way, shape or form later in the future."

I wanted to be the best at whatever I did which was a philosophy that would be instilled in me for the rest of my life.

As Boot Camp continued, we had what were called, *"Smoke and Cokes"* and as the name implied, it was a fifteen-minute break given to us periodically to smoke cigarettes and drink soda pop.

We took our *"Smoke and Cokes"* in the Canteen Area, which was located between our barracks and the barracks of Company 295, so we often took them together. The Canteen area was a fifteen by twenty foot room with tables and chairs, but also had vending machines which carried a variety of sodas.

We were allowed to go to a canteen area, light up and also buy drinks. At the time, I didn't smoke, so I just drank soda pop which was a treat during boot camp, because for eight weeks, you ate three square meals a day, but sweets and sodas were limited. Of course, there was also, no alcohol or drugs to be had, so for those who were accustomed to that lifestyle, they would suffer from withdrawal symptoms; boot camp certainly detoxified the body.

One day during a smoke and coke, I sat there and observed other guys light up and got curious. I thought to myself,

"Why do these guys get such a joy and pleasure out of smoking? Why did my mother used to smoke?"

My curiosity got the best of me, so I decided to ask for a drag off of someone's cigarette. I took a puff and got light-headed, not to mention coughed and gagged, but afterwards continued and finished up that cancer stick. I was officially hooked and now a smoker. I couldn't believe that I had picked up the habit that I had broken my mother from, but finally realized what all the hype was about. It was so relaxing and certainly put me at ease. I then wished that I had taken up the habit years ago. I could have used the sedation.

While I had picked up a new habit, I was also trying to pick up on some of the personalities of the guys in my company, but out of eighty-two young men, I only remember a few. Some people just leave a lasting impression on you and can never be forgotten.

Those people would be, of course Robert, our RPOC, who was eighteen years old, but very mature and more like a man than any man I knew of at that particular time. He definitely had the respect of the whole company. We listened to him and obeyed his every order.

Others included a tall, blonde haired, blue-eyed, all-American boy named Ryan. I must say myself that he was quite pathetic. You could tell he was a spoiled brat and probably born with a silver spoon in his mouth. He whined and acted like a baby all of the time. He had no physical stamina, no athleticism and actually dislocated his shoulder one day while doing calisthenics; no kidding.

Have you ever seen *"A Few Good Men?"* If you have, you will remember that the character Santiago was killed while being given a Code Red. In the movie, a *"Code Red"* was given to a Marine who may have been a sub-standard performer and always costing his fellow marines to endure more discipline and training than necessary. Well, Ryan was the *"Santiago"* of company 2-9-6.

I don't think he could do anything right. He couldn't march in step, he couldn't do calisthenics, he couldn't fold his personal effects the way they were supposed to be folded; he was a screw-up by all accounts. His blunders would cost him to get the naval version of a *"Code Red"*.

One night, I witnessed six other sailors hold Ryan down by pulling his blanket tightly across his body while he lay asleep in his rack. He slept in a top bunk, so that made it easy for him to be attacked.

With the help of the bright, outdoor, floodlights in the courtyard, I watched while three other guys placed a bar of soap in their respective net-type laundry bags and then wailed away at him with the homemade weapons. I could see him squirming and hear him yelling, but then someone covered his mouth while the other guys continued to hit him. He must have been hit at least ten to fifteen times before I started having flashbacks.

I remembered when my father woke me up in the middle of the night with a belt years before and how terrified I was. To be awakened out of your sleep with someone whipping you had to be one of the most horrifying moments of my childhood. As tears came to my eyes, I got out of my bunk and ran over to where Ryan was being brutalized.

"You guys need to stop this. Enough is enough; you need to stop!"

Again, I was the biggest guy in the company, so they stopped at my urging. After the guys let go of his blanket, Ryan jumped out of his rack and onto the floor while the sailors that were holding him down scattered in hopes that Ryan couldn't identify them.

"I'm going to tell UT1 on you guys," he cried, with puffy and teary eyes.

"Are you okay Ryan?" I said.

"No I'm not okay. That shit hurt. I am sore all over. Somebody is going to pay."

"Just calm down Ryan and go back to sleep, okay?"
"How do I know they aren't going to do that again?"
"Because I'm not going to let them, okay?"
"Okay, thanks Michael."
"You're welcome Ryan."
"Why are you crying?" Ryan asked me.
"I was just reliving a childhood moment, that's all. I'm okay," as I wiped my eyes.
"Well thanks Michael. I really appreciate your help."
"You're welcome. Are you going to be okay?"
"Yeah, I think so."

We both went back to bed and the rest of the night was quiet.

Ryan kept the beating to himself and had seemingly improved, but not enough. I don't think he made it through boot camp; he was asmo'd after only the second or third week. I didn't know what the acronym stood for. I just knew that it did mean that would be sent back to a more junior company in hopes that he could right the ship and eventually graduate.

Another person I remember was from Maine and his name was David. He had this really, strong New England Accent. He was seemingly always in trouble and UT1 disciplined him by having him doing push-ups.

"David! Drop down and give me twenty-five!"

"Yes suuh, right away suuh." David replied and then did his push-ups.

I heard that, "Yes suuh," for the first time and almost died laughing. It sounded so darn funny. I had never heard an accent like that before. I think UT1 had him doing push-ups and other things, just simply so he could here David say,

"Yes suuh, right away suuh."

David was a funny guy and to this day, his "Yes suuh." is as memorable now as it was the first day I ever heard it. I honestly don't know if he made it through boot camp either.

ME PLAYING AROUND IN THE BARRACKS

Chapter 28
A Different Kind of Smoker

Midway though boot camp, I had become the darling of the company. I was tough as nails on one side and somewhat of a perfectionist while making sure I did well on inspections. On the flip side of the coin, I was considered a big teddy bear. I was also known as the ultimate competitor.

It was for that reason I was selected by the company to fight in the Heavyweight Division of the *"Boxing Smokers"*. The *"Boxing Smokers"* was at the time, traditional boxing matches that the Navy held. I was against it at first, but was encouraged by others in my company to compete, so I did.

I was to fight this white guy named John in our sister company and it was cool because we were both well liked within our companies. We were also the biggest guys in our respective companies and to top it off, we both had Italian last names.

The hype built during the *"Smoke and Cokes"*, when everyone talked about what a great match it was going to be and who would win. More importantly, the company that won would also have bragging rights.

I had never been in a boxing ring before and for that matter neither had he, but on that day, we both faced off in the *"Navy Boxing Smokers"*. It was a three-round fight, lasting two minutes a round. We also wore sixteen-ounce gloves; the professionals wear eight-ounce.

During the first round we both just kind of jabbed while trying to feel each other out. After that round was over and while standing in my corner, I heard sailors from my company in the crowd,

"Come on Mike, get him! Knock him out Mike!"

I also remember those sixteen-ounce gloves feeling like sixteen pounds after only the first round. After the bell sounded to begin the second round, we got a little more aggressive, but with neither of us landing any significant punches. It was plain to see that we were novices. I swung very hard at times, but my own punches often landed me into the ropes instead of my opponent because I missed badly. The second round quickly came to an end and I went back to my corner when my company started the mantra.

"Ca-vi-can-te – Ca-vi-can-te – Ca-vi-can-te."

When the third round began, those doggone gloves felt like blocks of cement, but at the chant of my name, I got an adrenaline rush and went after John. I was throwing punches left and right while still missing most of them, but was by far the aggressor. I was so aggressive—that when John turned his back on me and ran towards the ropes, I advanced on him and sucker punched him in the head. He turned around and I went after him hard, but couldn't knock him out.

The final bell sounded and I was declared the winner. I am sure that it was only because I was the aggressor, not because I demolished him or anything. That sucker punch was the only one that landed cleanly, but I guess it was enough for the referee. My hand was raised in victory. I felt like Rocky and wanted to call out for Adrienne, but there was no Adrienne to be found, just my fellow sailors and that was enough for me. I was a champion and it felt great. John and I hugged in the center of the ring as everyone applauded.

I had a new respect, admiration and appreciation for professional boxers. They must be in superior physical condition to withstand the rigors of a boxing match.

I was in pretty good shape, but was completely exhausted at the end of the match. I got back to the barracks that night and was congratulated by the whole company. I felt like a star, but the jubilation would soon end. It was time to get back to basics.

We had just finished service week which is a week in which we were required to work in the Galley. It also meant getting up at four in the morning. What a grueling week that was.

After service week, we were able to do away with wearing our black knit-caps which is why we were called raisin-heads, because that was what they resembled. We had made it pass the halfway point and were able to wear our Dixie-cups, white guard belts and white leggings. Boy did we look sharp.

While marching, I loved when our RPOC made the command, *"Flying Mass Breakdown!"*

It was a command that meant instead of marching eight rows across, we had to reduce it in half, to four across; so the ranks would be longer, but narrower in order to navigate pass other companies. I can't speak for others, but when I heard my RPOC call that command, it gave me a woody because the entire company had to move with precision in order for it to work. One misstep would mess the whole formation up, so here goes.

"Flying Mass Breakdown! Second platoon, to the rear, march! To the right flank, march! To the right flank, march!"

I just so happened to be in the second platoon as first platoon didn't have to do anything except to keep marching forward; they had no flanking movements to make. Let me tell you, with our white leggings, white guard belts and Dixie cups on and doing a *"Flying Mass Breakdown"*, it had to be one of the most awesome feelings while in boot camp.

Other than my excitement over a variety of marching orders, there were inspections to deal with. Over the course of the grueling eight weeks, we had a lot of inspections, both as a company and personal. We had uniform inspections, barracks inspections, drill inspections, marching inspections. In boot camp, there were inspections for everything.

The reason for the inspections was two-fold. First, so you knew how you were supposed to dress, march, fold your clothes, and make your rack properly; secondly, because as a company, you were competing with at least ten other companies for best of the graduating class, so award points are accumulated as well as other awards, such as *"Big Chicken."*

I don't remember a lot of the company prizes that we received and being a superb company, we won a lot of them. It would figure that I would remember an award such as *"Big Chicken"*, because it had to do with my favorite pastime, eating.

I don't know exactly how we got *"Big Chicken"*, all I know is that when we had it, we were able to march to the front of the chow line while carrying the *"Big Chicken"* Flag, which meant that we didn't have to stand in line. It meant I could eat sooner rather than later, so I was especially happy when we got that award.

There were other awards that a company could win, but there were people in each company who could keep it from actually passing an inspection for

Michael Cavicante

several reasons. If you didn't make your bed (rack properly), if your blanket wasn't folded correctly and facing in the right direction, your shoes or belt buckle not being shined, your gig line not straight, not being clean shaved, dropping your weapon during arms inspection, or just simply moving while standing in ranks. Any of these things and more could fail you and/or the whole company and cost points which were called hits.

Over the course of Boot Camp, I watched other recruits be either ASMO'd, or be discharged all together for not being able to cut the mustard. If they weren't discharged or ASMO'd, there were others in my company that cost the company points/hits. But throughout over thirty inspections during boot camp, both company and personal, I never took so much as one hit or cost the company one single point or myself and was the model recruit sailor.

Company 296 would graduate and place second in the graduating group in total points, out of twelve companies. We would also graduate fifty-six of the eighty-two young men that started Boot Camp. Of course, I just so happened to be among the fifty-six that made it through. We graduated on Saturday, November second and what a beautiful November morning it was.

PACKING MY THINGS UP TO LEAVE BOOT CAMP

A Father's Double Life

Just before the graduation ceremony, I weighed in at a svelte two hundred two pounds. Okay, okay, I guess I was a little overweight.

UT1 gave me a hard time especially the whole time through. I think because I was the biggest guy in the company, so I guess he figured if he put me in check then he would have the respect of everyone else. That was his job, but in the end, he congratulated me and thanked me for being the model sailor.

For Graduation, we marched in parade with the rest of the graduating class while passing and saluting the Grandstand of Dignitaries. It was a proud day for me. For the very first time in my life, I felt part of something very, very special.

After graduation, I looked around in hopes that my parents would be there which was kind of an unrealistic expectation was considering their everlasting financial situation, but I thought that they might have made a way.

Though my parents weren't there—I was introduced to other sailor's parents and loved ones while I worked my way through the mob of people. I had made it through boot camp and was on my way to making a better life for myself.

I pondered my life and what I had been through so far. I had weathered the storm, a storm of poverty, my father's beatings, sexual molestation, foster homes, an overnight runaway, juvenile hall, injuries, disappointment, heartache, fights and rejection. There had been near death incidents—which probably could have included my father's beatings, cold nights in bed, a teenage circumcision, embarrassment, marijuana, alcohol, epilepsy, Phenobarbital, an insane asylum, working through high school, Twelfth Grade English and now, military boot camp.

As other sailors and their families brushed by me and as the crowd dissipated, I stood in the midst of it all and looked up into the heavens. A part of me wanted to cry, but I could only smile as I thought to myself,

"I am still standing and have defied all odds against me. I am now ready to conquer the world!! Bring it on!!

I then fade away into the crowd.

Michael Cavicante

THIS IS MY GRADUATION PICTURE FROM BOOT CAMP – THE SMILE ON MY FACE REPRESENTS THE HAPPIEST I HAD BEEN IN MY LIFE AT THAT POINT FOR I HAD MADE IT THROUGH THE STORM.

A Mother's Love
By
Juanita Maria Cavicante

HELLO TO THOSE OF YOU who have just read my son's story. I was against my son writing this novel, but after giving it heavy consideration, I realized that if it was going to bring him some closure, than I was all for it. When he was done though, I felt compelled to write some final words of my own and he agreed, so here goes.

I fell in love with a gorgeous, charismatic, charming and hard working man from San Francisco. I was so in love with him that I would have went to moon and back with him. He had those Hollywood good looks and a smile that you couldn't say no to. His hair was like silk and as I watched other women practically fall to their knees when he spoke to them, I knew that it was me whom he belonged to. I was so proud to have such a stud of a man, and that love continued for the most part, for years to come.

That love, would eventually come to a cease, when one night, I caught

Michael Cavicante

my son at the top of the stairs. He was crying like I had never seen him cry before. I just knew that all wasn't right with him. When he finally told me what had happened, I was totally in a state of shock. I must admit that I didn't believe him at first, but when I thought about the last couple of years prior to that night, it suddenly all made sense to me as my world suddenly came tumbling down.

I thought to myself that here was a son who was truly gifted and could do anything. He astonished me with his feats from an early age, as he was walking by ten months, potty trained by eighteen months and tying his shoes and completing full sentences before the age of two. By the age of three, he was practically taking care of his mentally challenged brother. He was truly a special child.

After moving to Memphis in 1969, he continued to impress. He was so obedient and hardly gave me an ounce of trouble, with the exception of the couple of instances he mentions in this story. Needless to say, the few times when Michael did screw up, he always did it grand fashion.

I knew that Michael was going to be picked on, because we were in the south and he was so different. He spoke very proper, never used profanity, was cute as a button and as sweet as could be, so it didn't surprise me that other kids picked on him.

Through elementary school, teachers raved about him and told me of his potential. He never gave them any problems and made good marks. But then came, the suspension from breaking the school window and the petty theft from a local store. I then wondered what the heck went wrong with my little boy.

On that fateful night when he gave me his story, I had finally figured it out. My son had been trying to deal with what my husband had done to him, for no kid changes like that without reason.

So when it dawned on me, I went downstairs into that bedroom and my husband and I had it out. He threw a glass ashtray at me, and if it hadn't been for me placing my hand up to block it from hitting my face, it would have severely injured me.

That particular night came to a tumultuous end and I have been celibate since. There was no way that I was going to let that man, or any other man, ever put his hands on me ever again.

As for my son, my beautiful son, he along with my other two kids was taken away from us. Even though it was for a little over fourteen months, it seemed like five years.

They weren't coming home from school, there were no meals to prepare

A Father's Double Life

and the house was silent. There were a couple of reasons that I stayed with him. First, because I was a woman who believed deeply in her vows and secondly; I knew that staying with him was the only way that I could get my kids back, because I had allowed him to strip me of my independence, as I had no means to support them on my own.

After they came back home, I was overjoyed. The hate that I once had for my husband slowly faded and I learned to forgive, but it didn't take away that pain that I felt for my son. My husband had lost his trucking job and eventually had a nervous breakdown. He worked odd jobs and was always hustling trying to put food on the table. He did have a lot of good qualities.

As time went on and we struggled, I watched Michael grow and mature into a fine young man. He was always willing to help me around the house as he washed the dishes as well as swept and mopped the floors. I wanted so much to be close to him, so much to the degree, that I even went and watched him during his football practices, because his father never went. I hated football and I hated even more what it could do to my son, but he loved the sport, so I supported him nonetheless.

When he started working at The Commercial Appeal, I wondered how he was going to ever graduate high school as his grades suffered immensely, and that was sad, because he was so bright. The one time he did make the Honor Roll amazed me, because I never saw him study or do homework. He just picked up things so easily, but the work load would just be too much for him.

He would get home at five-thirty in the morning, take a shower, eat breakfast and be at that bus stop at six-forty; he truly astonished me. On Wednesday's when he got his check, he would practically hand over all but a couple of dollars, and through it all, I never heard him complain one bit. What mother wouldn't adore and love a child like that.

It saddened me deeply when he went into the Navy, but it made me stronger. While continuing to work at The Commercial Appeal, I went to school and got my CNA License and then started working at the hospital.

I stayed with my husband, not because I loved him, but out of pity, as I realized that he needed me. Life was miserable, but I hung in there. I hung in there until the day he died.

Since then, I have known nothing but peace in my life. No, I have never had the material possessions that it is normal for the average person to long for, but I do have peace. I have peace knowing that my son, through all of his adversity, is doing very well.

When I visit him, I am in awe of the patience he shows, along with his wife, while raising their two precious kids. I admire how they look up to him and call him daddy and oh how blessed they are. I look around and see laptops, cell phones, x-boxes, flat screen televisions, ipods, and more. My son has certainly given them everything that he never had, but more importantly he gives them love.

I watch as he showers them with hugs and kisses them, while telling them that he loves them. All are things that my husband never did for Michael. My spouse was hard, while being very much the disciplinarian, but he made Michael tough in so many ways, which is probably why my son was able to endure so many heartaches.

Michael is such a beautiful person and takes very good care of me, always being there when I need him. He flew me and a friend to Florida and took me on a seven-day cruise for my seventieth birthday which I still talk about to this day, and most recently, took me to New York as we spent a week at a hotel in Times Square. It was my first ever trip to "The Big Apple".

What more can I say? Through it all, I can say that Michael, as well as my other two children, are true blessings. My son Robin lives with me, and though mentally challenged, gives me comfort in knowing that there is the man in the house. My daughter Wendy lives close by, and next to my Lord and savior, Jesus Christ, which is where I find my real peace; she also shares in being my guardian and protector.

I would like to thank you personally for reading my son's story. I personally think he told it very well, but then again, I'm his mother. I am going to have a biased opinion.

Take care and may God bless you as he has truly blessed me.

Hello my friend; I would like to thank you for purchasing my book and hope that you enjoyed my story. To read my Afterword as well as a final word from a close friend, please search Facebook for **"AFDL Afterword"**

You may also feel free to send me an email to cavicante41@yahoo.com and I will try to respond but can't make any promises. Please make sure to input, **"I read your book"** in the Subject line so that I will know it's from a fan.

You may also go to **Facebook** and become a FAN of either of my Fan Pages which are, "**A Father's Double Life – Autobiography**" and also make a comment about my book.

My other Fan Page is simply, "**Michael Cavicante – Published Author**" --- You may leave comments there also.

I thank you once again for reading my story hope you enjoyed it, but more so, I hope that it empowers and inspires you to achieve things that you never thought was possible as that was its main intention. I would hope that you would pass it along to someone whom you think it may help.

Take care and make sure to reach for the stars!! May God Bless and guide you in all of your endeavors!!!

References used for history;
Opening Chapter 1966 Facts – Wikipedia, The online Encyclopedia
Jimmy Carter Presidency - Wikipedia, The online Encyclopedia
Ronald Reagan Presidency - Wikipedia, The online Encyclopedia
Teddy Pendergrass - Wikipedia, The online Encyclopedia
Elvis Presley - Wikipedia, The online Encyclopedia

References used for movies and their history;
Star Wars Box Office Revenue – Yahoo Movies
Can't buy me love – From watching
Hardly Working – From watching
Uncle Buck – From watching
Ghost – From watching
Rocky – From watching
Roots – From watching

References to song history;
Michael Row the Boat Ashore – Wikipedia, About.com
Windy - Wikipedia, The online Encyclopedia
Fly Robin Fly - Wikipedia, The online Encyclopedia
Brick in the Wall – Memory of event
Tracks of my Tears – Wikipedia, the online Encyclopedia

Other online sources used were;
The Free Dictionary by Farlex
Merriam-Webster Online Dictionary
Thesaurus.com
Answers.com

The phrase that I use at the end of chapter one, "**It was plain to see that I wasn't in Kansas anymore**" was a phrase I wanted to use because it was similar to that of one of my all time favorite movies, "The Wizard of Oz."

Printed in Great Britain
by Amazon